ADULTS

Newham London

7/12

PUSHING THE ENVELOPE

MAKING SENSE OUT OF BUSINESS JARGON

CAROLINE TAGGART

Michael O'Mara Books Limited

First published in Great Britain in 2011 by
Michael O'Mara Books Limited
9 Lion Yard
Tremadoc Road
London SW4 7NQ

A CIP catalogue record for this book is available from the British
Library.

Papers used by Michael O'Mara Books Limited are natural,
recyclable products made from wood grown in sustainable forests.
The manufacturing processes conform to the environmental
regulations of the country of origin.

ISBN: 978-1-84317-651-0 in hardback print format
ISBN: 978-1-84317-771-5 in EPub format
ISBN: 978-1-84317-772-2 in Mobipocket format

1 2 3 4 5 6 7 8 9 10

www.mombooks.com

Illustrations by Andrew Pinder

Designed and typeset by K DESIGN, Somerset

Printed and bound in Great Britain by Clays Ltd, St Ives plc

Contents

Introduction 7

1 Considering your position 9
Getting a job, leaving a job and that awkward bit in between

2 Blue-sky thinking 36
Accentuating the positive

3 An executive decision 53
Gobbledygook from management and politicians

4 Mushroom management 75
How not to do it

5 The way forward 89
What the experts tell us

6 KSF in FMCG 113
Abbreviations and acronyms

7 Creative accounting 128
Money, its uses and abuses

8 At the click of a mouse 143
IT and the Web

9 Customer value orientation 158
Marketing speak

Acknowledgements 183

Bibliography 185

Index 187

Introduction

A friend approaching retirement was recently asked by a colleague if he was 'grooming an exit strategy'. Someone unfamiliar with modern idiom who overheard this conversation might well have wondered if my friend owned a horse, and if he was planning to commit suicide when he stopped work.

A teacher of creative writing described her students as 'bright, serious and **ENGAGED**'. 'Engaged?' our imaginary extraterrestrial might ask. 'To be married? All of them?'

The same alien, reading in the business columns of a newspaper, 'Working out the best **PACKAGE** can be complicated, as you can buy your broadband and landline separately or together, or buy a "**BUNDLE**" that also includes a digital television package', might be forgiven for thinking that he needed a supply of brown paper and string before he could invest in a home-entertainment system.

Jargon is an insider's language, a form of shorthand by which one member of a group communicates with another. Part of its bafflement is the way that it takes existing words and phrases and twists them for its own ends. But there is another side to it: the words and expressions that need to be coined in order to cope with new ideas. This gives us **AGILE DEVELOPMENT** and **MALWARE**, **CROWDSOURCING** and **MASS SAMPLING** – terms to cover concepts that didn't exist fifty years ago. Into this category might also fall the vocabularies of management consultants and marketing gurus, which produced **CORE**

COMPETENCIES, HORIZONTAL INITIATIVES and **MISSIONARY SELLING.** We understand the individual words. Put them together into phrases and we come up with ... well, some might say claptrap. But until recently it was still *insiders'* claptrap.

In the last decade or two, though, a funny thing has happened. Jargon has spread out from the specialist area in which it originated and permeated everyday language. Where once only a techie would talk about something being **IN THE LOOP** and only a politician would be expected to be **ON MESSAGE**, nowadays we are all at it. And much of the time, we don't have the slightest idea what it really means.

Current jargon may have its origins in a carnival parade (the **BANDWAGON EFFECT**) or a nineteenth-century children's novel (**WHITE KNIGHT**), the baseball field (**TOUCHING BASE**) or the internal combustion engine (**FIRING ON ALL CYLINDERS**). It may have been made up for fun (**WOMBAT**, short for 'waste of money, brains and time') or adopted because we are all so busy nowadays that we need to save nanoseconds where we can (**B2B, FACE TIME**). Some of it is imaginative, some annoying (no cross-reference here – just don't get me started). Some will pass into the language, some will disappear without trace once it has served its purpose.

The aim of this book is to shed a few glimmers of light on a cross-section of these expressions; to see where they came from and how they got to where they are today; and to translate the gobblydegook into plain English. It will sometimes be appreciative, sometimes irritable, but even at its grumpiest it will try to give credit to the versatility of the English language and to the people who keep pushing its particular envelope.

1

Considering your position

GETTING A JOB, LEAVING A JOB AND THAT AWKWARD BIT IN BETWEEN

There's jargon attached to interviews and recruitment and jargon attached to getting rid of people. There's also a lot of jargon attached to actually doing the job, whether it's sitting at your desk getting on with it, being positive at meetings or trying to keep in with your boss. This chapter considers some of the strange language we use to cover all these situations.

Brain dump

'To dump' in the sense of 'to copy data to another, usually external, location for security or back-up purposes' has been around since the 1950s, and it is this meaning that has been adopted into the 'brain dump'. It's a useful concept if you are leaving a job: you want to download everything pertinent that is in your brain and leave it in a form that your successor can absorb. However, lurking in the subtext of this expression is the idea that you are glad to be getting out, frankly past caring,

and the result is a haphazard collection of the sort of stuff you might have produced if you were interpreting the word 'dump' in quite another way. Or, indeed, if there were an **ELEPHANT IN THE ROOM**.

Brownie points

When I was in the Brownies, you didn't get points; you got badges for achievement in various fields such as cookery or starting campfires without endangering life and limb. No matter. Brownie points is the expression that entered the language about fifty years ago; to gain them means that in some way you have successfully sucked up to the boss and will be viewed more favourably from now on. Brownie points are nothing to do with **KPI**s or any of the other 'measurables' so beloved of management consultants (see **DASHBOARD**) – they are by definition nebulous and may be awarded or withdrawn at any time.

Close of play

One of only two expressions in this book to derive from cricket (see a **SAFE PAIR OF HANDS** for the other), this has been adopted into the working world to mean 'the end of the working day'. Which is, of course, what it means in cricket. Some people in the office context say 'end of play', making any cricket aficionados wince.

Considering your position

In business or politics, this is almost always followed by a resignation. Considering your position is something you have to do when the management has **MOVED THE GOALPOSTS**, **DOWNSIZED** your department or otherwise made it clear that they are thinking of **LETTING YOU GO**. If you are in the public eye, it is possible that you have done something scandalous and no one is prepared to **DRAW A LINE UNDER IT**. Whatever the circumstances, you are likely to be spending more time with your family in future.

Cubicle monkey

As early as 1682 a monkey could be 'a person engaged in any of various trades and professions, especially one performing a subordinate or menial task, or one which involves physical agility'. The oldest usage in this sense is 'powder monkey', meaning someone carrying gunpowder from the store to the guns themselves, particularly on a warship. Later there were grease monkeys, who mended cars and got covered in grease; bridge monkeys, who built bridges; and road monkeys, who repaired logging roads. In the US in the nineteenth century,

'monkey' was also thieves' slang for an associate or just a man, an unknown and uncared-about stranger. In Britain there was the organ grinder, whose less skilled companion was – literally – a monkey.

Take any combination of these attributes and remove the positive qualities of those born in the Chinese Year of the Monkey: liveliness, ambition, opportunism and entertainment value. Put them behind a low partition in an open-plan office and, hey presto, you have a cubicle monkey: an unappreciated functionary performing an endless stream of routine tasks. If you feel such a creature needs sustenance at any time, refer to the entry on **MUSHROOM MANAGEMENT** for advice on its diet.

Ducks in a row

In American bowling terminology, a duck or duckpin, first recorded in 1911, is 'a small pin shorter than a tenpin but proportionately wider at mid-diameter'. When you line such pins up – in a row – you are ready to bowl at them. If you do the same thing metaphorically, you have everything neat, tidy and organized. Your arrangements are completed, your in-tray and in-box are under control, your filing is done, goodness how your colleagues must hate you.

Elephant in the room

Here's an expression that has evolved in an interesting way over the last fifty years. The *OED*'s earliest citation, from the

New York Times in 1959, is 'Financing schools has become a problem about equal to having an elephant in the living room. It's so big you just can't ignore it.' However, in modern usage, the whole point of an elephant in the room is that you *do* ignore it. It's too big, too uncomfortable, too controversial to be other than pussyfooted around. Until, of course, you all realize that you are up to your necks in sh*t.

If, by the way, anyone looks blank when you suggest there is an elephant in the room, don't be tempted to tell them that this is an idiom. They're only waiting for the chance to ask whether the idiom elephant is the one with the small ears or the large ears.

Entry level

The earliest use of this dates from the 1950s and refers to the basic level at which a job or academic course may be entered and the minimum qualifications or experience required. At entry level, you might be given a job for which you had no obvious qualifications, perhaps because you were of **GRADUATE CALIBRE** and were deemed to have potential; in such circumstances you would receive suitable training or supervision rather than being expected to **HIT THE GROUND RUNNING**. From this, the use of 'entry level' has expanded to describe a product or activity suitable for a beginner: an 'entry-level computer' would be **USER-FRIENDLY** to the technologically challenged, while an 'entry-level adventure holiday' might suit someone who had never been white-water rafting before.

(Taking your) eye off the ball

This is a metaphor from the world of sport and clearly something that a SAFE PAIR OF HANDS would never do. First recorded in the 1930s, it means, of course, to let your attention wander, to lose sight of your objectives with results that are to a greater or lesser extent catastrophic. Taking your eye off the ball is not the same as batting on a sticky wicket, because the former is definitely your fault, the latter can be blamed on circumstances beyond your control.

Fast-track

The original 'fast tracks' were at racecourses where it hadn't rained lately and horses were able to run quickly over the hard ground. From there, by 1970, the expression had moved into the business world. It was initially used mostly as an adjective to describe an individual who was likely to be promoted rapidly or a training programme on which such a person might be put. Shortly afterwards it became a verb, so that bright children might be 'fast-tracked' by putting them up a year at school; drugs to combat highly publicized diseases (as opposed to ORPHANED ones) might be 'fast-tracked' on to the market; promising ENTRY-LEVEL office workers might be 'fast-tracked' into executive positions. You also see the word on signs at the passport-control and security areas of airports, where it simply means that those travelling business or first class – possibly people who live life in the fast lane – can jump the queue.

Fire-fighting

In the fire service, it's understood that fires are emergencies that need to be dealt with immediately. The same applies in other businesses, too, although the 'fire' may take a different form. It may be a computer bug, a breach in security or a crisis at the printer who is producing the catalogue for an exhibition that opens tomorrow. Serious problems arise when every day brings a new fire: there is no time for planning, consolidation, back-up or the implementation of strategy.

This modern meaning of fire-fighting – 'dealing with events as they occur, without long-term planning' – seems to have arisen as recently as the 1990s, perhaps in response to the **DOWNSIZING** of many corporations. At that time, those still in employment were routinely working ludicrous hours, doing both their own jobs and those of the people who had been **LET GO**, and finding that fire-fighting was the only way to cope.

The experts tell us that too much fire-fighting shows a lack of organization and risks drawing resources away from areas that are functioning perfectly well but that will now be sucked inexorably into the chaos. What is needed is **DRP**.

Gagging clause

Here's an unusual thing: an expression that is not a mealy-mouthed euphemism (see, for example, **GARDENING LEAVE**) but a gloves-off, no-messing piece of contractual terminology. Gagging or gag clauses may be found in a number of contexts, most notoriously in the now illegal US medical practice of not presenting a patient with all the options for treatment because some of them are deemed too expensive. The 'gag' was imposed on individual physicians by the Health Maintenance Organization that controlled their budgets. The ex-spouses and ex-nannies of celebrities may also find themselves bound by gagging clauses, preventing them selling their stories to the popular press.

In employment law, if you have a gagging clause in your contract, you are forbidden from revealing confidential information to journalists, competitors and the man on the Clapham omnibus. Careless talk costs jobs, in other words.

Gardening leave

A euphemism, in use since the 1980s, for sending someone home on full pay, normally to 'work out' a notice period without actually doing any work. In other words, you want rid of him, you don't want his pernicious influence round the office but if you sack him he'll sue. The implication is that he will have plenty of time to potter in his garden, which will keep him out of mischief and, specifically and often contractually, prevent him from selling his expertise to your competitors (see **GAGGING CLAUSE**). It's a bit like house arrest, with fewer guards. And more gardening.

Apologies for the sexist use of pronouns here: women may be sent on gardening leave too, but generally only if they have conquered the barriers of the **GLASS CEILING** and the **MARZIPAN LAYER**.

By the way, Americans call this 'garden leave'. As a nation they are perhaps less keen gardeners than the Brits, so it may be that those on garden leave are allowed to sit in theirs with a cool drink in their hands, rather than sweating over cutting the grass or weeding the flowerbeds.

Glass ceiling

An invisible barrier to advancement, usually applied to women and minority groups who fail to gain promotion beyond a certain level because (we assume) of their gender, ethnicity or other target for prejudice. Gay Bryant, author of

The Working Woman Report (1984), may have been the first to use the expression when she wrote:

> Partly because corporations are structured as pyramids, with many middle managers trying to move up into the few available spots, and partly because of continuing, though more subtle, discrimination, a lot of women are hitting a 'glass ceiling' and finding they can rise no further.

In the quarter-century since those words were written, increasing numbers of women have penetrated the glass ceiling only to find themselves bogged down in the **MARZIPAN LAYER**.

(Moving the) goalposts

The origins are obvious: moving the goalposts on a sports field makes it more difficult to score a goal. The *OED*'s earliest quotation (1958) suggests that the expression was first meant positively, as a way of stimulating students to set higher goals. Nowadays, moving the goalposts – whether political, financial or ethical – is almost invariably seen as unfair.

Golden handshake

All that glitters may not be gold, but there is certainly a lot of the glittery stuff being passed around when people change jobs. A golden handshake is a payout given to someone on retirement (as a reward for long and faithful service) or on leaving employment for some other reason (usually being sacked but having such a watertight contract that sacking without vast remuneration is not an option – see **GARDENING LEAVE**).

This concept was first recorded in 1960, to be followed some fifteen years later by the 'golden handcuff' – benefits, perhaps in the form of bonuses, share options or pension arrangements, that made it undesirable for a valued employee to leave. Then in the 1980s came the 'golden parachute', a guarantee of financial protection for senior management in corporations threatened with takeover, and finally the 'golden hello', another (inevitably substantial) sum paid to an already high earner, such as a company executive or a footballer, as an inducement to change jobs or clubs. Why this is not called simply a bribe is a matter for debate.

The recipient of a 'golden hello' is obviously a golden boy (or girl, though the **MARZIPAN LAYER** makes this less likely), but there is a warning attached to that sobriquet – it loses its lustre all too quickly. The term was coined in 1938 by the American playwright Clifford Odets, the central character of whose play *The Golden Boy* enjoys a brief flurry of success as a prize fighter. On his way to the top, however, his desire to win overpowers all the qualities that made him into a decent human being and he is eventually killed after he speeds off through the night in the flash car his winnings have bought him. If you've seen the film, starring William Holden, and remember a happier ending – well, that's Hollywood's golden age for you. And see **CASH COW** for a reminder of the dangers of killing the goose that lays the golden egg.

(Of) graduate calibre

This is an oddity, of recent coinage and often seen in recruitment advertisements. I call it an oddity because, short of putting a candidate through a degree course – surely too time-consuming a process for most businesses looking to employ bright young things – how do you decide if someone who doesn't have a degree is 'of graduate calibre'? Once upon a time advertisements would say something along the lines of 'The ideal candidate is likely to have a degree in ...', but perhaps in these days of KPIS and performance measurables the word 'likely' is just too frivolous.

Heads-up

A warning, given benevolently by one colleague to another, so that the latter can be prepared for something that is about to happen: 'I'll give you the heads-up on the sales figures before the meeting.' 'Heads up' was originally a military order, short for 'Lift your heads up.' This evolved into a more general expression of encouragement, now perhaps less common than 'Chin up', meaning 'Be brave, don't let it get you down.'

From here, originally in the US, 'heads-up' developed into an adjective meaning 'competent, in the know': 'She was a very heads-up teacher, always looking for new ways of interesting the children.' Thence, by the 1970s, still as an adjective, it came to mean 'in the form of an advance warning': 'A heads-up memo was circulated to a chosen few before the news was made public.' The current usage, as a noun, is recorded in the early 1980s.

◆

Hitting the ground running

Be afraid when you hear this phrase in a job interview. Be very afraid. The company, or at least the area you are being invited to join, is in chaos. It is understaffed and underorganized. There will be no training. There will be no handover period with the previous incumbent, because he or she has been **LET GO** as a result of causing the chaos in the first place. There will be no suggestion of breaking yourself in gently, finding your

feet or feeling your way. You will be expected to know the job inside out from the word go. Did I mention that you should be afraid?

Used in a literal sense this expression – as when someone leaps off a train and makes a dash for it – dates back more than a hundred years; the figurative sense is found in the 1960s and like many business metaphors it is billed as 'colloquial, originally US'.

Knee-jerk reaction

If you are sitting down with your feet off the floor and someone taps you just below the knee with a small hammer, the lower part of your leg jerks forward. Physiologically, this is a knee-jerk reaction – a reflex action that you don't make consciously and can't easily prevent. Also called the patellar reflex, it's been known in medical circles since the early nineteenth century and is a good thing because it means the tendons that control the knee are functioning properly. In business and politics, however, where the expression has been used since the 1960s, a knee-jerk reaction is generally a bad thing: a reaction made automatically, without thought, in a 'We always do it like this' sort of way. **IF IT AIN'T BROKE, DON'T FIX IT** may be a sensible, pragmatic approach; a knee-jerk reaction is plain lazy.

Letting (someone) go

Except on television reality shows, almost no one is fired these days. At least, not in so many words. Being let go is the business equivalent of being told by a boyfriend/girlfriend, 'It's not you, it's me' or 'I just need a bit more of my own space.' Wrap it up in fancy linen as much as you like, you are still being dumped. Similarly, 'We're going to have to let you go', 'We need to adapt our staffing levels to current market conditions' or anything that has the word **DOWNSIZING** in it all boil down to the same thing: you're on the way out.

(A) level playing field

Playing on a level field is like knowing where the goalposts are (see **(MOVING THE) GOALPOSTS**): it makes the game a whole lot easier and fairer. As with **TOUCHING BASE**, there is no early recorded example of the expression being used literally; it sprang fully formed into the world of metaphor in the 1970s. So ingrained in the vocabulary has it become that there is now a Level Playing Field Institute, based in San Francisco, whose vision is 'a world where everyone has access to opportunities, including the historically disenfranchised' – in other words, 'a world where a true level playing field exists'. Among other things, LPFI offers a Summer Math And Science Honors academy (SMASH) and an Initiative for Diversity in Education And Leadership (IDEAL). So, highly commendable though its vision obviously is, the institute is not above contorting the names of its courses to produce improbably positive acronyms.

Marzipan layer

A recent coinage, credited to Sylvia Hewlett of the Center for Work-Life Policy, to describe the sticky area just below boardroom level above which few women manage to rise: although there are many accomplished women in not quite the top jobs, only 3 per cent of the Fortune 500 corporations (the 500 largest in the United States) have female CEOs. Sylvia maintains that this is because women lack the 'sponsorship' of powerful people (usually men) who will back them all the way.

Having an affair with the boss is, apparently, commonplace among women at this level and sometimes leads to advancement, but does nothing to endear the woman concerned to colleagues of either sex. Think it over, girls – do you want everyone who works for you to bitch behind your back about how you got the job? See also **GLASS CEILING**.

Methodology

At the start of a thesis or other academic paper, it is traditional to detail what you were setting out to establish, how you collected and analysed your data, how this enabled you to draw your conclusions, why this was the best way of going about it. This is a methodology. So important is it in academic circles that there are innumerable websites offering students advice on how to write one clearly and accurately.

What a methodology *isn't* is a method. So to say, 'When preparing a presentation, my usual methodology is to make notes, expand on the key points, then throw in a few jokes' is to use jargon of the worst kind. In a world where saving fractions of a second seems so important to so many people (see **FACE TIME**) it is surely crazy to use a word of five syllables when a word of two would not only do perfectly well, but would be more accurate and less pretentious.

Mindset

A mindset started out as much the same as 'a set mind' – a fixed attitude or way of doing things. Used by psychologists from the early years of the twentieth century, it moved into common parlance by the 1960s. But it has since been taken up by life coaches, who – as is their wont – have put a positive SPIN on it. Nowadays the right mindset can ensure that you are successful at work, happy at home, vice versa or both. From being an inflexible barrier to development, it has become something that can itself be developed to make you into the dynamic, charismatic person you always knew you were really.

Package

You might think that a package would be the same as a bundle (see BUNDLING), and so in a sense it used to be: a 'package holiday' offered several services in one – flight, hotel, car hire, excursions. Nowadays, however, 'package' has turned into an abbreviation for two very different things, the equivalents of a golden hello and a GOLDEN HANDSHAKE. As an inducement to join a company you might be offered an attractive 'package' – not just salary but health benefits, generous paid holidays and so forth. When times are tough and they need to LET YOU GO, your 'package' means a redundancy package. See also DELAYERING.

27

Pushing someone's buttons

Not exclusively a business term, this, as you can push the buttons of your nearest and dearest too. The idea of pushing a button to make something like a doorbell work has been around since the late nineteenth century; the suggestion that a person had buttons which, when pushed, would not merely annoy them but would really really touch a nerve seems to have evolved as early as the 1920s. However, like ETA (particularly in Portugal), this is an expression that should be used with care in the workplace: 'pushing someone's buttons' can also mean to turn them on, in the sexual sense – and charges of harassment have been brought for sillier reasons.

Raising the bar

This has its origins in high-jumping and pole-vaulting: after each round of a competition, the bar is raised so that the remaining contestants have to jump or vault ever higher. Since the 1970s it has been widely used in a metaphorical sense to mean to aim for a higher standard. It's possible, also, to lower the bar, but not many people in business would admit to that.

Raising your game

Unlike **RAISING THE BAR**, this is not deliberately setting yourself a new challenge. Instead, the new challenge has been set for you and you have to play (or, in the metaphorical sense, work) that little bit better and harder in order to achieve your goals. I say goals, but in fact the earliest uses of the expression refer to the goalpost-free game of tennis. Maybe the idea was that you hit the ball a bit higher so that it didn't flop into the net. Anyway, the expression had spread into the business world by the 1980s.

(A) safe pair of hands

In sport, this is definitely a complimentary description: it originates in cricket and describes a fielder who is unlikely to drop a catch. It's been used in this context – and with reference to rugby players and footballing goalkeepers, two other roles in which catching ability is important – practically since the games were invented. Its non-sporting use, from the 1980s or so, generally applies to business or politics. Again it is usually a compliment: a person so described can, to put it bluntly, be trusted not to screw up. On the other hand, it can be a bit like saying someone is nice, because there is nothing more exciting to say about them. A safe pair of hands is never going to set the world on fire. For that, you need **MOVERS AND SHAKERS**.

Self-starter

In the employment world, a self-starter will **HIT THE GROUND RUNNING** and be able to **FIRE ON ALL CYLINDERS** without the need for **MICRO-MANAGEMENT**. In other words, a salesman will be capable of picking up the phone and approaching potential new clients; a journalist will have ideas for stories; a dressmaker will know how to thread a needle and cut out a piece of fabric. However, the moment the person has entered employment the expression will be dropped: it is almost never used outside 'situations vacant' columns.

Like firing on all cylinders, the image comes from the early days of the motor car, when a vehicle with a self-starter was more sophisticated than one that had to be cranked with a starter handle. The figurative use has been around since the 1960s, the decade when initiative and individuality were prized above all other qualities.

Shooting the puppy

In his book *Shoot the Puppy*, Tony Thorne, Language and Innovation Consultant at King's College London, traces this expression's origins to the 1980s US gameshow producer Chuck Barris. Chuck apparently speculated about how desperate people were to appear on television and came up with a fantasy format that involved asking members of the studio audience to shoot a puppy out of the arms of a small child. What he wanted to know was, 'How *little* money would people accept to do this appalling thing, just to gain those few seconds of fame?' For some reason this format was never made into a long-running series, so we can only continue to wonder about the answer to Chuck's question.

Moving on from this inauspicious start, shooting the puppy means 'taking the most extreme action imaginable' when, to quote Tony Thorne again, things have gone 'several steps beyond "grasping the nettle" or "biting the bullet"'. In a business context it can be a positive thing – making the really tough decision that just has to be made – but is very much the last resort, to be taken after **DOWNSIZING** and **GOLDEN HANDSHAKES** have failed.

(Up to) speed

This started life in the nineteenth century as a literal expression, used of a racehorse or a motor car running at full speed, or at least as fast as you could reasonably expect it to go. By the 1970s 'to bring someone up to speed' was a substitute for 'to brief them, fill them in on the latest developments' and so it has remained. It's not dissimilar to keeping someone (**IN THE**) **LOOP** in the hope that they will (**GET WITH**) **THE PROGRAMME** and be (**ON**) **MESSAGE**.

Synergy

This has meant 'working productively together' for several hundred years, but it went through a number of specialist meanings before re-emerging into the world of jargon. Muscles synergize to produce a required action in the body; a combination of drugs synergizes to become more effective than any one of them would be individually. But nowadays –

and from as long ago as the 1950s – a group of colleagues or business partners can combine to produce synergy. What you or I might call 'better results'.

Time poor, cash rich

This was the great cry of the over-worked, over-stressed 1980s when it seemed that lots of people had plenty of money but no time to spend or enjoy it. How times change. And, as one encyclopedia of management wryly points out, being time poor but cash rich tends to be a lifestyle choice: those who are time poor and cash poor because they work hard in badly paid jobs rarely have any say in the matter. See also **WORK-LIFE BALANCE**.

Touching base

This translates as 'ringing up to say hello because we haven't been in touch for a while' or 'attending the same meeting, ostensibly in order to maintain close contact but in fact so briefly as to be almost pointless'. The expression dates from the early twentieth century and, surprisingly, there is no previous recorded use in a literal sense from the world of baseball. But that is where it originates: a batter must touch a base as he runs round the diamond, so if he is hoping to score a home run he passes each base very quickly and with only the most token 'communication'.

Water-cooler moment

It was once the hallmark of a television programme's success that 'everyone' was talking about it in the office next day. Cynical programme makers were even alleged to insert controversial incidents specifically to make this happen. Although the discussion traditionally takes place round the water-cooler, it can happen equally efficiently over the coffee machine, by the photocopier or in the smoking area outside the back door.

The expression is first recorded in the 1990s and took off shortly afterwards, when it became a running gag in the comedy series *Seinfeld.* By that time, with so many channels for viewers to choose from, the concept of 'everyone' watching the same television programme was on the way to being obsolete, but I guess you couldn't have water-cooler moments until most offices had water coolers.

Anyway, details of chronology and water temperature apart, the point of a water-cooler moment is that, although it is discussed in the workplace, it by definition involves no work at all.

Workshop

Formerly a place where physical work such as carpentry was done, this became from the 1930s a meeting in which the participants took an active role. Early workshops tended to be in the arts, and writing workshops (often promising 'a friendly, supportive atmosphere') are still advertised in every writers'

magazine. But workshops are now an integral part of management training: you can attend workshops in team-building, communications, motivation, planning and goodness knows what all besides. 'Participation and involvement increase the sense of **OWNERSHIP** and **EMPOWERMENT**,' claims one website, emphasizing the most important aspect of any workshop: you aren't allowed just to sit there and doze, or even just to sit there and take notes. That won't help your team-building skills one bit.

2

Blue-sky thinking

ACCENTUATING THE POSITIVE

It sometimes seems as if the worst thing you can do in business is the same thing as you did yesterday. This chapter aims to celebrate and inspire those to whom **IF IT AIN'T BROKE, DON'T FIX IT** is anathema and who can't get through the working day without a good **CAFFEINE-FUELLED BRAINSTORMING** session.

Blue-sky thinking

… is one of many expressions in modern business designed to encourage people to **PUSH THE ENVELOPE, THINK OUTSIDE THE BOX** and make the most of any **WINDOW OF OPPORTUNITY.** In fact, in the early days – the 1960s and '70s – blue-sky thinking was something to avoid: it meant pie in the sky, unrealistic, ignoring such minor difficulties as 'the technology hasn't been invented yet' or 'we don't have the money'. However, the mood of caution of the late twentieth-century seems to have been abandoned in the current climate, so that blue-sky thinking has come to mean 'the sky's the limit, let's go for it'.

Hang on. A mood of caution has been abandoned in the current climate? That can't be right. Would any of you people up in the wild blue yonder care to think again?

Brainstorming

This term is often considered non-PC these days, presumably because the original meaning of a 'brain storm' was a sudden disturbance of the mind, a 'mental explosion' which might take the form of severe headaches or temper tantrums. In about the 1950s it was adopted into non-medical vocabulary to mean 'thrashing out ideas through intensive, impromptu discussion', but in 2004 some over-zealous new recruit to the Thought Police decided that it was offensive to those suffering from epilepsy.

The National Society for Epilepsy promptly and commendably carried out a survey which reported that '93 per cent of people with epilepsy did not find the term derogatory or offensive in any way and many felt that this sort of political correctness singled out people with epilepsy as being easily offended'. So that's one in the eye for the Thought Police. Result.

A stronger argument against using the expression is, surely, the possibility of confusion: in the UK, 'I had a brain storm' tends to be said apologetically, meaning, 'I had a fit of mental aberration', whereas in the US it is more likely to mean 'I had a brainwave', which would render a brainstorming session superfluous. If the word offends you, for whatever reason, try having a 'thought shower' instead – although on the face

37

of it meaningless, it's clean, quiet and probably uses less hot water.

Caffeine-fuelled

Caffeine is 'an alkaloid that occurs naturally in tea, coffee, cocoa and cola nuts, acting as a mild stimulant to the nervous system'. In other words, it's the ingredient in coffee in particular that gives you a bit of a kick and can help keep you awake long enough to finish the task in hand. Caffeine-fuelled is most often used somewhat pejoratively with reference to teenagers who, unable to sleep because of all the coffee they have consumed, stay up into the small hours texting and tweeting to their friends. Which, when you come to think of it, adds a rather sweet 1950s innocence to the use of twenty-first-century technology: does anyone really think that drinking coffee is what they have been doing all evening?

The expression has now drifted over into the work context and taken on a more positive tone, so that a caffeine-fuelled meeting is one where everyone has taken in suitable quantities of legal stimulants and is buzzing with bright ideas. Enabling them to PUSH THE ENVELOPE, THINK OUTSIDE THE BOX, yadda yadda ...

Covering all (the) bases

'Protecting against any eventuality': a term from baseball, in which a fielding player stands close to a base, ready to catch the ball if it is thrown to him and so be more likely to get the opposing player out. If all the bases are covered, the batting side is in a difficult position. In the business world, where the expression popped up in the 1990s, it is assumed that you belong to the fielding side: by covering all the bases you are keeping your head well below the **PARAPET**. See also **TOUCHING BASE**.

Cutting edge

Obviously knives have a cutting edge and the figurative use of the expression to mean 'a dynamic factor that gives an advantage' has been around since the middle of the nineteenth century. Cutting-edge technology, which came along a hundred years later, metaphorically cuts through barriers and produces innovative ideas that put it at the forefront of its field. Nowadays it is not only technology that is cutting-edge: the expression can be applied to, among other things, cinema or theatre, art and, since Heston Blumenthal appeared on the scene, cooking.

The foremost edge of a propeller blade, which does much of the work of shifting an aircraft forwards, is called a *leading* edge; if you prefer to take your metaphors from aviation (as you may, if you are in favour of **PUSHING THE ENVELOPE**) you can substitute this for 'cutting edge' without changing your meaning. Or, if your innovations have fallen flat and you feel that a period of consolidation is called for, you can replace either expression with 'bleeding edge'; in the UK at least, most people will realize that you are being satirical.

Downshifting

Not to be confused with **DOWNSIZING**, this is a voluntary action on the part of an individual or family wanting to achieve a better **WORK-LIFE BALANCE**, accepting lower pay in order to work fewer hours and/or in a less stressful job. It is satirized as meaning moving to Wales or Vermont to keep chickens, but doesn't have to be that drastic: it could just mean moving to a smaller house in the same neighbourhood. In the nineteenth century 'downshift' could refer to any downward movement; by the mid-twentieth it was applied to downward trends in the stock market, consumerism or other money-focused areas. The specific modern meaning evolved at the same time as the concept, around the 1980s.

Firing on all cylinders

An internal combustion engine that is in optimum working order is said to fire on all (possibly four, possibly six) cylinders. The figurative use of the expression to describe someone being particularly efficient or brilliant is first recorded in the early years of the twentieth century and was well established by 1932, when P G Wodehouse wrote, in his novel *Hot Water*, 'His smiling face, taken in conjunction with the bottle of wine which he carried, conveyed to Gordon Carlisle the definite picture of a libertine operating on all six cylinders.'

In the business context, this is not the only cliché to be inspired by the internal combustion engine. Someone who is firing on all cylinders may well cause sparks to fly, be described as a dynamo or, if he is just too full of bright ideas, cause his colleagues to blow a gasket.

Fit for purpose

Does it (whatever 'it' may be) do what it is meant to do? If so, it is fit for purpose. An early use of the expression is found in a tome with the comprehensive title of *The Law-Dictionary, explaining the rise, progress and present state of the British Law, defining and interpreting the terms or words of art and comprising also copious information on the subjects of trade and government.* In the 1835 edition, a lengthy explanation of the contractual obligations of a 'carrier' contains the words, 'A carrier by water contracting to carry goods for hire impliedly promises that the vessel shall be tight and fit for the purpose, and is answerable for damage arising from leakage.' 'Tight' in this context means 'water-tight', and the sentence puts into legalese the not unreasonable assumption that, if you are hiring out a boat, it mustn't be likely to sink.

By the 1860s the 'the' had been dropped from 'fit for the purpose' and it is the shorter form that has come down to us. The expression remains mostly British and was repopularized in 2006 when the then Home Secretary John Reid described the immigration directorate, which fell within his remit, as 'not fit for purpose' following a series of scandals involving illegal immigrants. To be fair to Dr Reid, he had at the time of that speech been Home Secretary for less than a month. Indeed, serendipitously for the purposes of this book, Wikipedia tells us that when he arrived at the Home Office he **HIT THE GROUND RUNNING**.

Joined-up

A description made notorious in the UK in the early years of this century by New Labour's 'joined-up government'. Efforts to define it have not always been entirely successful. The following is a quotation from a working paper produced in 2007 by the State Services Authority of Victoria, Australia, which gives 'horizontal, holistic or integrated government and whole of government' as synonyms for the term. It then proceeds to explain:

> Whole of government denotes public service agencies working across portfolio boundaries to achieve a shared

goal and an integrated government response to particular issues. Approaches can be formal and informal. They can focus on policy development, program management and service delivery.

And, in case that isn't clear, the report goes on to say, 'Joined up government is generally focused on improving outcomes.' Which raises the interesting question, what do you call a government that is focused on making outcomes worse?

To be less cynical, the concept is a perfectly sensible one: that some public policy issues are too complex to be slotted into a single portfolio but require co-operation between various departments. Not rocket science, you might have thought, but then many concepts that aren't rocket science seem to have fancy names these days. See **TECHNOLOGY MIGRATION**, to name but one.

Leading edge

See **CUTTING EDGE**.

Learning curve

Why a curve? Well, think back to school maths and visualize the sort of graph where you plotted one set of values along the x axis, another along the y and joined all the dots into a curve. (Didn't do that at school? Pity. This entry will be wasted on you.) Anyway, from the 1920s on, a graph like this was used by

43

educationalists and psychologists to illustrate someone's progress in learning. The x axis (along the bottom of the graph) conventionally indicated the time elapsed since the subject started school or entered employment, the y axis (up the left-hand side) their level of competence. The steeper the curve, the faster they were learning.

Some time in the last twenty years or so, this technical term was annexed into informal language, so that 'It was a steep learning curve for me' means 'I had to learn a lot, quickly, and it was hard.' Or, as people who use this sort of jargon would say, 'challenging'.

(On) message

'In accordance with the ideas and policies of the political party, company, etc to which you belong.' The meaning encompasses both an individual toeing the party line and the party being able to get its message across, possibly through the prudent use of SPIN doctors, media consultants and the like. Employees who are not 'on message' may be encouraged to **(GET WITH) THE PROGRAMME** – or face the ignominy of being LET GO or sent on GARDENING LEAVE. The expression emerged in US politics in the early 1990s and found its way to Britain shortly afterwards.

Nerve centre

A term from biology meaning a group of nerve cells from which individual nerves branch out and which is involved with a specific function. The figurative use, to denote the central point from which information or control flows ('the Senior Common Room is the intellectual nerve centre of the college'), dates from about the 1980s.

(Get with) the programme

This is very much American in origin, so it is often written '... with the program', although there is no connection with computing (the only context in which the word is spelt this way in British English). It originally meant 'to do what you are supposed to do': in a 1974 episode of the TV series *Columbo*, military trainees are woken at an ungodly hour with the cry, 'Up and at 'em; let's get with the program' – it is time for them to get on with their duties, working through the day's schedule. From this practical application the expression has been adopted into the workplace to mean 'to make a positive contribution, to be on top of things', with the implication that you believe in and are prepared to go out and promote the company's ethos. See also **(ON) MESSAGE** and **CORPORATE DNA**.

Punching above your weight

Professional boxing is organized so that the two contenders in a bout are much the same weight (bantamweight, featherweight, heavyweight etc.). A fighter 'punching above his weight' is taking on a heavier man and acquitting himself well. The idea moved out of the boxing ring into the wider world in the 1980s, so that now a small company 'punching above its weight' may be achieving surprisingly good results in terms of sales, market share or publicity.

A recent review of a children's book described it as 'punching above the usual picture-book territory and introducing serious topics, such as homelessness, for discussion'. The fact that the reviewer could get away with using an incomplete form of the expression shows that it is being integrated into the language as an idiom whose original meaning is on the way to being forgotten.

Pushing the envelope

In aeronautical terms, the 'flight envelope' is an aeroplane's best possible performance – a combination of fastest speed, highest altitude, farthest range, etc. Engineers or test pilots who pushed the envelope were trying to extend these limits, to produce a plane that would fly faster, higher, farther. The American author Tom Wolfe is credited with having popularized the expression in his book *The Right Stuff* (1979), but he didn't invent it – he quotes it as something that pilots said. Within a decade of Wolfe's using it, pushing the envelope had expanded beyond the field of aeronautics and was being applied to any pioneering endeavour that made the undoable doable or the unacceptable acceptable. See also **BLUE-SKY THINKING** and **THINKING OUTSIDE THE BOX**, and contemplate a bad joke heard somewhere: 'No matter how much you push the envelope, it'll still be stationery.'

Quantum leap

To a physicist, a quantum leap is 'the sudden transition of an electron, atom etc., from one energy state to another' – a concept far too complex to go into here. To everyone else it is a spectacular advance, often skipping an intermediate stage that had previously been thought of as vital. So in physics, it is a significant but tiny thing, carried out at a subatomic level. Everywhere else it is huge.

The German physicist Max Planck first identified the quantum in the early years of the twentieth century and won the 1918 Nobel Prize as a result; by 1930 physicists had given it the ability to leap and by the 1950s the idea was infiltrating the worlds of politics and business. See also **PARADIGM SHIFT**.

Singing from the same song sheet/hymn sheet

This is sometimes also described as 'being on the same page' and means working from the same assumptions and towards the same goals. Checking at an early stage that everyone is singing from the same song sheet avoids costly and acrimonious misunderstandings later. Obviously the reference is to members of a choir, whose singing will descend into chaos if they don't all have the same music in front of them. The idea of a number of people 'singing the same song' or 'the same tune' – that is, expressing the same opinion, particularly in public (and possibly suppressing their personal views in the interests of apparent unity) – is recorded in the mid-nineteenth century; the use of a 'sheet' belongs to the second half of the twentieth.

To give an example from the business world, under the headline 'Is everyone singing from the same song sheet?', the website solutionsforsales.com sensibly points out that a sales organization has to persuade customers and potential customers that buying from it is a sound business decision. This can't be done 'if the various people they come into contact with are all telling them a different story … If you can't deliver a consistent message then you disappear into the background noise.' In this context, the song sheet is the framework on which your **OFFER** is built, the means by which you convey its meaning to your **STAKEHOLDERS** and the way you ensure that everyone on your sales team is (**ON) MESSAGE**.

State of the art

The first process recorded as being 'state of the art' is photographic printing; the expression dates back to the 1880s. Since then it has been in constant use for anything that scientific or technological skill can produce. In modern parlance this tends to be electronics (a 'state of the art' HD television or 3G smartphone) or scientific and particularly medical equipment ('state of the art' computer-aided diagnosis). Whatever it is, you can be quietly confident that it looks impressive, was expensive and you'll be wanting to replace it this time next week.

Thinking outside the box

Did anyone ever think inside a box? It must have been an uncomfortable thing to do. But this expression emerged in about the 1970s, when sending executives on courses became fashionable (management training courses had been in existence since the 1930s, but kept a lowish profile for their first few decades). The received wisdom is that thinking outside the box comes from a test of lateral thinking, popular around this time. The subject is given a piece of paper on which there is a square containing nine dots; he or she is then asked to join the dots using four straight lines, without lifting pen from paper. Human nature, being the unimaginative thing that it is, assumes that the lines must be drawn inside the square. But no. The inventive, lateral-thinking, management-potential participant recognizes that it is impossible to achieve the desired result unless you think (and draw lines) 'outside the box'. Aha!

Thinking the unthinkable

This sounds as if it ought to be deplorable, like **SHOOTING THE PUPPY**; in fact thinking the unthinkable is a positive, imaginative thing to do. Which is odd, really, because in the early 1960s 'the unthinkable' meant nuclear war. The American strategist Herman Kahn popularized the expression with his book *Thinking About the Unthinkable* (1962) and was at the forefront of the policy of Mutually Assured Destruction – the idea that the only way to prevent a nuclear attack was for the US to make it clear to the Russians that they too would be blasted to smithereens. Herman, by the way, was a student

of game theory (see **ZERO-SUM GAME**), but it doesn't sound as if he would have been much fun to play with.

The expression took on a new lease of life in British politics after Tony Blair became Prime Minister in 1997 and allegedly asked his Minister for Welfare Reform, Frank Field, to 'think the unthinkable' with reference to the benefits system. Although subsequent events have cast doubt on what Mr Blair intended, it seems safe to assume that he didn't mean 'drop an atom bomb on it'. By 2001 the expression was familiar enough to lend itself to the title of a radio sitcom in which a team of clueless management consultants, Unthinkable Solutions, advised clients to implement weird and inevitably disastrous policies, and lampooned pompous management speak while they were at it. If you can hear a rustling in the corner, it is Herman Kahn turning in his grave.

Thought shower

See **BRAINSTORMING**.

Work-life balance

In the mid-1990s some half-million people in Britain were believed to be suffering from work-related stress. Everyone – not just high-powered executives and working mothers – seemed to be reading their emails in the shower first thing in the morning in a desperate effort to keep up and sending emails at eleven o'clock at night to show their boss that they had true commitment and were still on the case when they should have been in bed.

So that just had to go. In its place came work-life balance. The expression was first recorded in 1977 but became part of daily language and angst-ridden newspaper articles only after the **INFORMATION OVERLOAD** brought about by email. It means people having a measure of control over when and how much they work, though the website worklifebalance.com wisely points out that there is no 'perfect, one-size-fits-all' balance that everyone should strive for. It's up to you to decide where your priorities lie and how they might change at different phases in your life. In other words, are you happy to earn less in order to be able to relax more or would you rather work yourself into an early grave in order to rake in an obscene salary? See also **EMPOWERMENT** and **TIME POOR, CASH RICH**.

3

An executive decision

GOBBLEDYGOOK FROM MANAGEMENT AND POLITICIANS

It's the job of management and government to see the **BIG PICTURE**, to have a long-term strategy for the company or the country. They may not always explain that to the rest of us and they sometimes have to make hard decisions along the way.

Benchmark

Online journalist Ian Dunt wrote recently, 'There is ... a strict minimal benchmark of material possession, under which political freedoms become irrelevant. After all, what use is the right to privacy if you have to sleep on the streets?' It's a good point and we all know what he means, but why a *bench*mark?

Unusually for business speak, the term comes from surveying and meant originally 'a mark on a post or other permanent feature, at a point whose exact elevation and position are known'. Given that fixed point, you can – if your maths is up to it – calculate the elevation and position of other points. And what about the bench? Well, a benchmark was of a clearly defined shape, a broad arrow with a horizontal bar through it, and surveyors inserted an angle-iron into the bar, forming, according to the *OED*, 'a temporary bracket or *bench* for the support of the levelling-staff, which can thus be placed on exactly the same base on any subsequent occasion'.

From this the term broadened to mean a criterion in any field, a known point against which other things can be measured. Even this figurative sense dates back to the nineteenth century.

Big picture

In the early days of the cinema the 'big picture' was the main feature, the one starring people you had heard of, as opposed to the low-budget 'B movie' that might be part of the same afternoon's entertainment. Since 1935 it has also been 'a broad overview of a situation, a way of identifying overall aims and strategy'. The boss – the one with the vision to see where the company will be in ten years' time – is a 'big picture' person. He or she doesn't need or want to be bothered with details. It is up to the team at the next level of management down to find ways of implementing the policies and to carry out the business on a day-to-day basis. However, if these people take their attention to detail too far, it will come under the heading of **MICRO-MANAGEMENT** and irritate their **DIRECT REPORTS**.

Broad brush

There is no recorded use of this expression in the art world, but obviously if you paint with a broad brush you are not going to produce much detail and you'd be rubbish as a *pointilliste*. (All those little dots? Not for me, thanks.) Similarly an executive who deals in broad brushstrokes does not go in for **MICRO-MANAGEMENT**. Around since the 1960s, this image can be approving or disapproving: after all, one person's visionary interest in the **BIG PICTURE** is another's careless lack of attention to detail. It all depends on where you are **COMING FROM**.

Corporate DNA

For a living being, DNA is a combination of all the myriad elements that make us the individuals we are. For a corporation, it is much the same thing: core values, ethos, the invisible but fundamental aspects that make it unique. The *OED* records a use of deoxyribonucleic acid from a scientific journal of 1944, although 1953 is the most famous date in the history of DNA: that is when Watson and Crick discovered the 'double-helix' structure. It was fifty years later that the business world took the idea to its corporate bosom.

Dashboard

This used to be the panel behind the steering wheel that showed you how fast you were driving and when you needed more petrol (even before that, it was a mudguard on a horse-drawn vehicle). Then it became that handy application on an Apple computer that included a clock, a calendar, a calculator and the weather forecast. Now it has been co-opted by management consultants, leading to claims such as 'the top management dashboard is an effective means to monitor strategy execution and predefined objectives achievement. The dashboard structure definition, the selection of adequate KPIs and their visualization are the key elements of this step.' Knowing that KPIs are Key Performance Indicators will help you translate some of this into English, but only some of it. In a nutshell, it's about measuring performance in the workplace – something that performance-measurement consultants think is important and most other people regard as substantial five-figure sums down the drain.

Wikipedia helpfully tells us that dashboards should not be confused with scorecards. Is this a mistake, do you think? Should it be dartboards?

Downsizing

At the time of the 1970s oil crisis, Americans, for the first time, were encouraged to drive smaller and more economical vehicles, and car manufacturers began to produce 'downsized' models. Early uses of the term are very specific, talking about 'shedding 6.5 inches of wheelbase' and increasing the amount of aluminium used in order to make the vehicles lighter. By the 1980s, however, the sense had branched out from the automobile industry to include anything that might be made smaller, including a business. It wasn't long before that meaning was transferred from the business itself to the person who might be 'downsized' or LET GO when the company tightened its metaphorical belt. The *OED*, in a draft addition dated March 2006, describes this usage as 'frequently euphemistic or humorous'. Events in the global financial sector since that date may have led many people to think that it isn't as funny as all that.

(Let's) draw a line under it

…'and move on' is the spoken or unspoken conclusion here. You have made a mistake, have lost any **BROWNIE POINTS** you may have accumulated but you are not – this time – being **LET GO**. The expression originates in accountancy, where drawing a line under a calculation indicates that it is finished with and something fresh is to be begun. Continuing with that metaphor, if you are offered the chance to 'draw a line under it' you may turn over a new leaf and start with a clean sheet. But – to move away from the accountancy imagery and into the real world – you should nevertheless watch your back.

Executive decision

This has its origins in nineteenth-century American politics, where it meant 'a decision made by the Executive' (that is, the President's office) or by someone with executive power in their particular realm. For the last half-century or so it hasn't meant much more than 'decision' and doesn't need to be made by an executive. But it does carry a certain amount of subtext: 'I am going to make an executive decision' suggests that the subject has been discussed long enough and there is never going to be complete agreement. It is therefore time for somebody (it doesn't much matter who) to decide on a course of action that enables everyone to move forward. Ideology has failed to carry the day, so pragmatism must take over. In fact, in most contexts you could substitute the word 'arbitrary' for 'executive' and not change the meaning appreciably.

Front-line services

They had front lines in the First World War, and doubtless in many wars before then: self-explanatory, they were the places where you were most likely to get shot. If you had done front-line service and survived, you had earned your medals. In spades. You can also have front-line states, adjacent countries that are hostile to one another; the term was frequently applied to war-torn parts of the Middle East and Africa in the mid- to late twentieth century.

But then 'front-line services' became a buzzword in British politics from about 2009: they were the services that were to be protected from cuts. Sadly, no one seems to have a clear definition of what they are (perhaps the government does? Who can tell?). The original theory seems to have been that bureaucrats, expensive R & D projects and pen-pushers would be expendable, whereas those who did real work – not only doctors, nurses, teachers, police and fire fighters, but those who met the public and/or got their hands dirty in a variety of jobs – would be safe. At the time of writing, it is difficult to say anything more definite than 'Hmm.'

It may or may not be a coincidence that Frontline is also the brand name of a product widely used on cats and dogs for the treatment of fleas.

Game plan

American footballers have had game plans since the 1940s and the expression soon spread out into the wider world: it means little more than a plan, a way of achieving your ends. It can be of almost any duration: you can have a game plan for the company over the next five years, or just to get you through this afternoon's meeting.

Guidelines

A guideline was once drawn on a piece of wood to show the sawyer where to saw, or used on a template to show a designer or typographer how the words should line up on a page. It could also be a rope hung from a hot-air balloon or small aircraft to help with steering. Figurative guidelines, such as moral ones to keep us on the straight and narrow, have been around since the mid-twentieth century. Since the invention of the nanny state, however, government guidelines have turned this perfectly reasonable word into a cliché: we now have guidelines on everything from school homework to alcohol intake, and it can be only a matter of time before they feel the need to warn us to finish the one before starting on the other. There are government guidelines on the amount of exercise we should take, on how local councils should handle sensitive data and on whether we should breast- or bottle-feed our babies. Perhaps we should draft in the Royal College of Midwives to advise on the economy.

Hands-on/hands-off

In the late 1960s, when avant-garde companies had a computer room with one vast computer in it and less avant-garde ones were still doing sums, by no means everyone could have direct experience of using the technology. Those who were able to sit down at a keyboard gained hands-on experience; the rest were lucky if they were given a copy of the manual to read. Use of the term has broadened greatly since then and you can have hands-on experience of almost anything, whether or not it involves using your hands: by the 1980s a company in Brisbane was advertising 'hands-on marketing **WORKSHOPS**', suggesting that participants would do

Watch out, he's a hands-on director.

something other than sit and listen to a lecturer (tautologically, surely, as participation is the key point that distinguishes a workshop from a lecture). From here 'hands-on' developed to be a compliment to a manager who was prepared – normally metaphorically – to get his or her hands dirty, to become involved in the practical aspects of a job, rather than sitting behind a desk and worrying about the **BIG PICTURE**. The hands-on approach can, of course, be taken too far: see **MICRO-MANAGEMENT**.

Surprisingly enough, 'hands-off' came into existence via a different route. In the early years of the twentieth century a 'hands-off policy' was any policy of non-intervention, whether prompted by laziness or the result of a considered course of action. The arrival of aviation brought the concept of 'hands-off' controls into the dictionaries in the 1930s. But 'hands-off' management seems to have been created in about the 1990s as the opposite of 'hands-on', with no specific reference to automatic pilots.

(Playing) hardball

'Using tough, uncompromising tactics in order to achieve your own ends'. In the nineteenth and occasionally the twentieth centuries, hardball (spelt variously as one or two words or with a hyphen) was another name for baseball, for the not-rocket-science reason that it was played with a harder ball than softball. Aficionados of softball tend to be children, women or non-serious athletes; 'real men' play baseball because, in the literal sense, they can cope with the harder ball and, in the figurative one, they can deal with the tougher approach. The metaphor has been around, mostly in North America, where the game and its vocabulary are endemic, since the 1970s; 'to hardball' emerged a decade later.

Horses for courses

If you are a fan of horse-racing you will often hear television pundits remark that one horse will do well with fast going (see **FAST-TRACK**), whereas the owners of another are hoping that it will rain overnight so that the ground is heavier. By extension, one horse may always seem to do well on a particular course which, for whatever reason, is suited to its style. In the business world, the same can apply to either a policy or a person – the former adapted to fit the circumstances, the latter chosen because he or she is suited to them. Racing correspondents were using this expression in the 1890s; the figurative sense came not long afterwards and was an established usage verging on the cliché by the 1960s.

Keeping your options open

Not committing yourself to a course of action until you are sure it is the right one is all very well, but can an option, an act of choosing, be open? The expression has been around for half a century, but where did it come from?

No one seems sure, but the most satisfactory explanation derives from the subsidiary meaning of 'option' as 'a right to conclude a financial transaction within a specified period': a stockbroker may take an option on certain shares, or a film producer may 'option' a book that he may or may not later make into a film. The key here is that the decision to act must be made before a certain date: if you keep an option open you extend the deadline.

In the less formal, less strictly financial sense, it may, of course, simply mean that you don't know the answer yet and are trying to fob people off until you do.

Lose-lose situation

See **NO-WIN SITUATION**.

Mission statement

This expression was originally a military one, referring to the objective of a particular 'mission' or task; it had moved into the business world by the 1980s, becoming a rather grandiose alternative to 'what this company does'. The Center for Business Planning goes further in the grandiosity stakes: it says that a mission statement should be 'a clear and succinct representation of the enterprise's purpose for existence. It should incorporate socially meaningful and measurable criteria, addressing concepts such as the moral/ethical position of the enterprise, public image, the target market, products/services, the geographic domain and expectations of growth and profitability.'

It's difficult to imagine how you can cover all that ground and still remain succinct, but perhaps that is part of the challenge.

Monitoring the situation

In the early twentieth century, radio (and later television) transmissions were monitored: it meant checking the technical quality without interrupting the service. During the Second World War, the word acquired an undertone of espionage, or at least of security: you might monitor (= eavesdrop on) a conversation or monitor a convoy of ships (to see where they were going and what they were up to). The more general use gradually evolved in the post-war years, so that now 'monitoring the situation' means 'keeping an eye on it, to make sure it runs along smoothly'. It is, in a business sense, a perfectly reasonable thing to do, not to be confused with 'keeping the situation under review', which has a pussyfooting ring to it and is more closely related to KEEPING ONE'S OPTIONS OPEN.

Movers and shakers

These are the dynamic, active people who get things done. Unusually, we know exactly when this expression was first used: in a poem called *Ode* by Arthur William Edgar O'Shaughnessy, published in 1873. According to Arthur, the 'music-makers' and the 'dreamers of dreams', 'world-losers

and world-forsakers' are 'the movers and shakers of the world forever, it seems'. 'One man with a dream' can achieve anything he sets his heart on, while the people who have no vision sit around and wait for someone else to tell them what to do.

No-win situation

... is one in which – self-evidently – there is no possibility of anyone winning. It was first used in political circles in the 1960s, at about the same time as game theory (see **ZERO-SUM GAME**) was producing the happier win-win and less happy lose-lose situations. All three soon spread into the wider world.

Pan out

... as in 'We'll see how it pans out', meaning 'We'll see what happens'. It sounds like a laissez-faire approach to business, but this attitude may be taken in the hope of striking gold. The expression comes from gold-mining days, when miners washed quantities of soil in a pan in the hope of leaving nuggets of gold behind. The first use – in the literal sense – dates from the California Gold Rush of the 1840s; in 1870 an early figurative use is attributed to Mark Twain, who wrote to his publisher, 'January and November [sic] didn't pan out as well as December – for you remember you had sold 12,000 copies in December ... But $4,000 is pretty gorgeous. One don't pick that up often, with a book.' Considering that, according to one Consumer Price Index calculation, $4,000 in 1870 would equal $152,000 now, one sure don't. But as the book in question was the recently published *Innocents Abroad*, which became Mark's bestselling book in his lifetime and is still one of the bestselling travel books ever, you never know how these things are going to pan out.

Paradigm shift

A paradigm is an exemplar, a stereotypical example. American author Robert Shea once wrote, 'Military organization, like religious organization, can be seen as a paradigm of organization in general', which is a rare example of this much-abused word being used accurately. In the philosophy of science it also means the broad concept within which a certain enquiry is undertaken. A paradigm shift is therefore a change in the concept or **METHODOLOGY** of such an enquiry. In the 1970s the term began to move away from the philosophy of science, into the world of technology and beyond. Over the years, inevitably, it has become debased: in a context such as 'the industry is at a crisis point and a paradigm shift is required', paradigm has become simply a posher sounding alternative to 'fundamental'.

Parameters

A parameter's origins are mathematical: in geometry, it once meant a chord in a circle, specifically (according to the *OED*) 'the latus rectum, the chord bisected by and perpendicular to the transverse axis'. You can see why that might not have caught on. By the nineteenth century it had developed a number of technical meanings in fields as wide-ranging as astronomy and crystallography, but in most cases it meant (roughly) a measurement that helped you to take other measurements. It had also, by the 1960s, been taken up by the music world. According to the musicologist Joan Peyser, Robert Beyer, a pioneer of the use of electronics in music production, borrowed the term from mathematics 'apparently to give weight and dignity to what otherwise would be called an element or dimension'. From there 'parameter' has been adopted into common parlance to give weight and dignity to what might otherwise be called **GUIDELINES**: rules or restrictions imposed by schedule and budget.

(Above/below the) parapet

A parapet was originally a chest-high wall, the sort of thing designed to stop you falling off a balcony. By the sixteenth century it had become a similar-sized defensive mound placed in front of a trench or built at the top of a fortification to prevent arrows raining in. Obviously, if you raised your head above the parapet you were more likely to have it shot off.

It works that way in politics and business too. In the last forty years or so the concept of 'raising one's head above the parapet' has been used in such circles to mean 'exposing oneself to scrutiny'. The prudent politician keeps his head below the parapet and, as the late Conservative MP Sir Julian Critchley so wisely put it, confines his pleasures to a bag of boiled sweets.

(In) real terms

This started life – in the mid-twentieth century – as an economic concept, meaning what money could actually buy, rather than any nominal or theoretical value. For the non-economists among us, the *OED* gives this example from 1976: 'NDP leader David Lewis ... calculated that Canadian business receives about as much in federal subsidies as it pays in federal income tax – and thus contributes practically nothing, in real terms, to running the government.' Since that time the expression has penetrated so far into day-to-day business speak as to be practically meaningless: 'What are we doing, in real terms?' means very little more than 'What are we doing?', though it does perhaps imply an element of 'Cut the crap, won't you?'

Ring-fencing

A ring fence was originally – from the seventeenth century – a fence that went all the way round a property, enclosing it completely; by the nineteenth century the term was being used figuratively to mean any barrier that protected something completely or preserved it for a specific purpose. The expression became a cliché of British politics after the arrival in 2010 of the Coalition government and its spending-cuts hatchet: promises were frequently made that budgets for – oh, say, the health service, pre-school education, school sports, foreign aid, whatever the politicians' audience wanted to hear that day – would be ring-fenced; that is, whatever was to be cut, it wouldn't be the thing that you and your vote cared about. See also **FRONT-LINE SERVICES**.

Sitting down

Jargon at its absolute rock-bottom silliest: 'Shall we sit down on this?' means 'Shall we have a meeting about it?' and may be said even if all concerned are already sitting down and in a meeting.

Spin-offs/spin-outs

Spin-offs came first: from the 1950s, they were shares in a new company distributed to the stockholders of a parent company; thence the expression came to refer to the new subsidiary company itself. From there it was applied to people setting up on their own having left a larger enterprise or, in a less clearly defined sense, benefits or discoveries emerging from a technological development: Teflon, for example, can be regarded as a spin-off from research into CFC refrigerants. Call it a by-product, a side-effect or an accident if you prefer. The specific usage to describe a new TV series centring on some of the same characters from an old one, as *Joey* was a spin-off from *Friends* or *Torchwood* from *Doctor Who*, evolved from this sense and emerged in the 1960s.

Spin-outs, meaning exactly the same thing, came into being in the 1970s; the connection with a vehicle spinning out of control on a racetrack or a slippery road may be coincidental and is certainly unfortunate.

Squaring the circle

Geometry specialists through the centuries have tried to create a square that has the same area as a given circle. Why? I have no idea. Perhaps they liked the process's formal name, which is quadrature. Anyway, in the nineteenth century somebody managed to prove that it was impossible. It's to do with the transcendental nature of pi, as I'm sure you knew. So, while the mathematicians may have given up trying, the expression has been adopted into real life to mean 'any impossible task'.

Stand up and be counted

Standing up and being counted is a bit like lifting your head **(ABOVE THE) PARAPET** – it means admitting what you believe or where your sympathies lie, and being prepared to take the consequences. There was a time, particularly with reference to electioneering in the US, when voters or anyone else wanting to make their views known had literally to stand up, but not any more. You've been able to stand up and be counted without moving out of your chair since the early years of the twentieth century.

Swarm intelligence

'Were I fortunate enough to be Miss Prism's pupil, I would hang upon her lips,' says Canon Chasuble in Oscar Wilde's *The Importance of Being Earnest*. Then, realizing that the spinster governess thinks this is perhaps a touch intimate, he adds hastily, 'I spoke metaphorically. My metaphor was drawn from bees.' The metaphor of swarm intelligence is also drawn from bees: it means lots of people working together, as in a hive or an ant colony, to a common end, without any one individual knowing what the **BIG PICTURE** is. It began life in the late 1980s in a specialist field of artificial intelligence and soon spread out, through the medium of science fiction and the *Matrix* films, into the wider world. You can also have swarm factors and swarm logic and although no one really understands them, they are generally a bad thing. We'd have no honey in the world without them.

Talk the talk, walk the walk

Sometimes abbreviated to 'walk the talk', this is not a million miles from 'put your money where your mouth is'. But in a good way. To talk the talk is to convey company policy articulately and convincingly if not necessarily sincerely. To *walk* the talk is to put it into action, particularly when it comes to 'ethical, values-driven leadership'. As Eric Harvey, founder of walkthetalk.com, puts it, 'People hear what we say, but see what we do … and seeing is believing.'

Win-win situation

See **NO-WIN SITUATION**.

Zero-sum game

... is a situation in which the gains and losses add up to zero: the winner can gain no more and no less than the loser loses. So this is neither WIN-WIN nor NO-WIN, but something in between. Think of noughts and crosses: every cross A adds to the game brings B closer to losing; every nought B puts in does the same for A. It also works on the stock exchange, where gains in the futures market depend on someone else losing.

The expression originated in game theory, a branch of applied mathematics whose influence extends to economics, international politics and many other fields (including noughts and crosses and the stock exchange). One of the theory's most famous exponents is the mathematician and Nobel Prize-winner John Nash and, if you think you have never heard of him, cast your mind back to the film *A Beautiful Mind:* John Nash is the character played by Russell Crowe. Oh yes, I can hear you murmuring. Game theory. I remember now.

4

Mushroom management

HOW NOT TO DO IT

In the last chapter we tried to give management the benefit of the doubt: they were doing their best, bless them. In this chapter, all such charity is thrown out the window. This is the bosses getting it wrong.

Bandwagon effect

A bandwagon (spelt sometimes as two words, sometimes with a hyphen) is something you jump on. Originally and literally it was the wagon that carried a band of musicians during an American parade; you might jump on it because it looked such fun and you were carried away by your enthusiasm. It sounds like something Tom Sawyer might have done, and it dates from about that period – the late nineteenth century. In business, the bandwagon effect describes something that is done simply because others are doing it: publishing gloomy thrillers set in Scandinavia, perhaps, or producing little pots of yoghurt that promise to lower cholesterol (only as part of a healthy diet and lifestyle, though – always read the small print).

The bandwagon effect is said to be particularly influential in American politics: someone who is rated highly in the polls will attract more votes simply because he is rated highly in the polls. The Brits, with their love of the underdog, don't fall for that quite so readily. But we still buy lots of those little pots of yoghurt.

Blamestorming

A recent coinage and an obvious spoof on **BRAINSTORMING**, this is a meeting or discussion intended to establish why something went wrong. It goes without saying that all concerned are trying to avoid responsibility and blame someone else. Now that some say we aren't supposed to use 'brainstorming' any more, it's tempting to wonder whether 'fault showering', by analogy with 'thought showering', might be a logical development. Or, in the legal world, perhaps 'tort showering'.

Bleeding edge

See **CUTTING EDGE**.

(I know/see where you're) coming from

This is capable of at least two interpretations, depending on the tone in which it is spoken. In both instances it means very little more than 'I see what you mean', but can either be dubious – almost certain to be followed by 'but ...', as with **I HEAR WHAT YOU SAY** – or meditative. 'Hmm, I know where you're coming from' is the nearest some bosses get to 'Wow, that's a good idea.' Even if your proposal is then implemented and turns out to be a great success, you are advised not to hold your breath waiting to receive the credit for it.

I hear what you say

This irritating remark is almost invariably followed (aloud or *sotto voce*) by 'but I disagree with every word of it' or 'I am going to ignore it entirely'. The participants in this unsatisfactory conversation are generally boss and underling, with underling objecting to some unpopular action or policy and boss digging his heels in. Speaking these words, however, enables the most stubborn of bosses to persuade himself that he is operating an **OPEN-DOOR MANAGEMENT** policy and has participated in a full and frank exchange of views with his **DIRECT REPORTS**.

If it ain't broke, don't fix it

We used to say 'leave well (enough) alone' – don't meddle with something that is working perfectly well, because you'll probably do more harm than good. 'If it ain't broke, don't fix it', which means much the same thing, is said to have been around in the rural parlance of the southern United States for some years before it was popularized by Thomas Bertram Lance, Director of the Office of Management and Budget under President Jimmy Carter. Bert, as he was known, was quoted in a 1977 newsletter of the US Chamber of Commerce:

> Bert Lance believes he can save Uncle Sam billions if he can get the government to adopt a simple motto: 'If it ain't broke, don't fix it.' He explains: 'That's the trouble with government: Fixing things that aren't broken and not fixing things that are broken.'

In the same year Bert was involved in a financial scandal that inspired the journalist William Safire to write a Pulitzer prize-winning piece entitled 'Carter's Broken Lance'. Bert resigned soon afterwards, perhaps taking the view that there was no point even attempting to fix his political career.

Micro-management

Giving absolutely no thought to the BIG PICTURE, micro-managers manage every paperclip and coffee cup. Their subordinates have no opportunity to use their discretion or even just to get quietly on with their jobs. The expression has been around – and driving its victims crazy – since the 1970s.

Mushroom management

Not normally advocated as a serious course of action, this means 'keep employees in the dark and feed them bullshit'. Slang supremo Jonathon Green's *Dictionary of Jargon* (1987) defines 'mushroom theory' slightly differently: 'a theory of management that tacitly considers that the best way of treating employees is to "put them in the dark, feed them shit and watch them grow".' This surely suggests that the outcome will be positive, a view with which most disgruntled employees muttering, 'Sometimes I think I'm a mushroom ...' would disagree. The *OED*'s earliest reference is dated 1989, but refers to the 'familiar philosophy of mushroom management' – and certainly the idea of disgruntled employees muttering under their breath has been with us since some poor minion had to drag the wooden horse inside the walls of Troy.

◆

Nibbled to death by ducks

Harvard professor Stephen Walt, writing in the first six months of Barack Obama's presidency, worried that the new president's foreign policy would meet with unfulfilled promises of co-operation from various other nation states, making it very difficult to implement. The policy therefore ran the risk of failing 'not because he loses some dramatic confrontation, but simply because a whole array of weaker actors manage to grind him down. In this scenario he doesn't get vanquished, just "nibbled to death by ducks".'

It's a bit like SALAMI TACTICS. No single dreadful thing happens, but the end result is still a cancelled project, a slashed budget or constructive dismissal. Ducks don't have teeth, but they can deliver a powerful – and damaging – suck.

The earliest use of this expression I can find is in the title of a crime novel by Robert Campbell published in 1989. Mr Campbell, Oscar-nominated Hollywood scriptwriter as well as novelist, had a penchant for animal-based phrases: *Nibbled to Death by Ducks* is one of a series whose other titles include *The Cat's Meow*, *The Gift Horse's Mouth* and, alarmingly, *Hip Deep in Alligators*. The fact that his publishers thought *Nibbled to Death by Ducks* was a saleable title suggests that it was an established phrase by the time he submitted his manuscript.

One-trick pony

Not much of business speak originates in the circus, but this is the exception to that rule. A one-trick pony, as early as 1905, was a poor sort of circus performer – a pony that could do only one trick. In the business world, the expression has been applied to companies and individuals since the 1990s and refers to, in the former case, a company that produces only one halfway-decent product or, in the latter, a person of limited abilities who is at a loss outside their own specialist area. You might have thought that knowing your area of expertise and sticking to it would be a good thing, but not in this instance: being a one-trick pony is not going to earn you either respect or promotion.

Reinventing the wheel

... is by definition an unnecessary thing to do, as the wheel was invented at least 5,500 years ago and was known to civilizations across Europe and Asia. Yet there are always those who don't trust the work of their predecessors or colleagues and to whom the words 'pragmatism' and 'just get on with it' are unknown. They waste time, effort and resources running round in circles (appropriately enough, given what they are trying to reinvent) in order to arrive – exhausted, deadlines missed and budgets exceeded – exactly where they started from. The expression has been around since the 1950s; the concept, to the hair-tearing frustration of those who *do* understand pragmatism and getting on with it, is timeless. See also **WOMBAT**.

Revolving-door policy

If you walk into a revolving door from the outside of a building and keep pushing, you quickly end up outside again. If your business is going down the pan and you lose one CEO after another, you may be accused of having a 'revolving-door policy', suggesting that the CEOs don't have time to come in and take their coats off before being escorted out.

Revolving doors were invented in the late nineteenth century; the term has been transferred to the business world only recently, though of course the idea that CEOs don't know whether they are coming or going is as old as time. The principal advantage of a revolving door is that it reduces draughts; what its effect is on hot air is a matter for conjecture.

Salami tactics/salami technique

Salami tactics, perhaps surprisingly, have their origins in Hungary. Or perhaps it is not surprising, on second thoughts, as salami features prominently in the Hungarian diet. (They spell it *szalámi*, but then they call food *élelmiszer* and pork *disznóhús*, so *szalámi* is one of their easier words.) Anyway, in the middle of the twentieth century, Hungary's ruling Communist Party was led by an unpleasant-sounding individual called Mátyás Rákosi. According to a 1952 edition of *The Times*, he described one stage in his rise to power as '"salami tactics", by which slices of the Small-holders' Party were cut away and its strength worn down'. In other words, the people of Hungary woke up one morning to find Mr Rákosi in undisputed charge, because his removal of the opposition had been so subtle that nobody noticed until it was too late.

It seems to have been the Americans who took this softly-softly approach one stage further and developed the salami *technique*: 'a type of computer fraud in which small amounts of money are transferred from numerous customer accounts into an account held under a false name'. The idea is that if you embezzle little enough from enough people, again nobody will notice. On the other hand, your illicit bank balance will mount up very nicely thank you and you'll be inundated with requests from people wanting to spend their holidays in your villa in the Cayman Islands.

Ticking boxes

The idea of ticking (or, in the US, 'checking') boxes derives from questionnaires and multi-choice tests in which no original thought is required: the answers are in front of you, you merely have to pick the most appropriate (or, in the case of some magazine quizzes, the least inappropriate) one. The modern version of this is to click on the box saying, 'I have read and understood the terms and conditions ...', when everyone knows you have done nothing of the sort.

Deriving from this comes the depressing activity familiar to many **CUBICLE MONKEYS**: going through the motions of work, being seen to do what the bosses or the government require without actually achieving anything worthwhile.

Trickle-down

It may look like a verb, but trickle-down is more commonly used as a noun or an adjective (as in 'trickle-down effect'). The idea is that something which benefits the higher (usually = wealthier) sectors of society or of a corporation will eventually benefit the poorer elements too. It's a concept that seems to have arisen in the US in the 1930s and has since been much pooh-poohed by the poorer elements who are still waiting for their circumstances to improve. As early as 1949 President Harry S. Truman dismissed it; in his State of the Union address he maintained that:

> During the last sixteen years [i.e. since my party has been in power], our people have been creating a society which offers

new opportunities for every man to enjoy his share of the good things of life. We have rejected the discredited theory that the fortunes of the nation should be in the hands of a privileged few. We have abandoned the 'trickle-down' concept of national prosperity. Instead, we believe that our economic system should rest on a democratic foundation and that wealth should be created for the benefit of all.

Well, that was only in 1949: it's early days ...

Waiting for the other shoe to drop

In the business context, the 'other shoe' normally signifies a second wave of redundancies: survivors of the first swathe of the scythe wait nervously to lose their own jobs and – in what has been described as 'other shoe syndrome' – become so unproductive that the cost savings made by the original cutbacks are wasted. According to Eric Partridge in *A Dictionary of Catch Phrases British and American* (1977), the expression derives from a story about a lodging house. A lodger in an upstairs room routinely dropped his shoes loudly on the floor, one after the other, every night when he went to bed. His downstairs neighbour complained, but the next night the upstairs lodger dropped the first shoe as usual. Then he remembered that he had promised not to do this any more. When he removed his other shoe, he put it down on the floor gently and quietly. After a long pause, the downstairs neighbour, who had been lying awake all this time, yelled, 'For God's sake, drop the other shoe!'

Wake-up call

This used to be what you got in a hotel catering for business travellers, when you asked the clerk at the front desk to ring you at an obscenely early hour. Nowadays, you can programme the phone in your room to perform the same service, so wake-up calls have become figurative. Instead of jet-lagged executives, the recipients are usually management or politicians whose bad results – in an interim report or a by-election, perhaps – should alert them to the fact that their current course is likely to end in disaster. In other words, wake-up calls no longer say, 'Good morning, madam, it's 5 a.m.' They say, 'Do something about it. Now!'

Worst-case scenario

It means 'if the worst happens', but that is the sort of clear, no-nonsense English that has no place in today's business world. This is now such a universally recognized set phrase that many people say merely 'worst case', leaving their audience to supply the rest.

The expression was familiar enough in 1999 for Joshua Piven and David Borgenicht to have a spectacular success with their *Worst-Case Scenario Survival Handbook*, which contains such invaluable advice as how to escape from quicksand, fend off a shark, deliver a baby in a taxicab and survive if your parachute fails to open. All of these scenarios suggest that – assuming Joshua and David are writing from experience – they are running far too many unnecessary risks and should either stay at home and take it a bit easier or look very closely at their insurance policies. Or both.

5

The way forward

WHAT THE EXPERTS TELL US

When all else fails, businesses bring in management consultants to show them what to do next. Opinions vary hugely as to how much value for money is delivered on these occasions, but one thing cannot be denied: they bring a whole new vocabulary, and a whole new meaning to many everyday words.

Action

On the basis that 'any noun can be verbed' and also that a saving of nanoseconds is of value in business speak, this has come to be preferred to 'put into action' or 'act upon' in contexts such as actioning tasks that need to be completed or actioning decisions that were made at a meeting. Although purists purse their lips and maintain that this usage is yet another sign that the world is going to hell in a handcart, the *OED* has an example dated 1960 and another from Len Deighton's *The Ipcress File* (1962). If it's good enough for Michael Caine, it's good enough for me.

Oh no, on second thoughts, it isn't. It's hideous. Sorry, Sir Michael.

(Get into) bed (with)

An expression, and indeed a concept, that needs to be used carefully if you don't want to find yourself making headlines in a tabloid newspaper. It means – appropriately enough – 'form a (probably casual and unofficial) partnership with', though it may also be used of a formal merger. More like a marriage, in fact, though probably one of convenience. Although we tend to think of most business jargon as being coined in the 1970s or '80s, the *OED* records an American use as early as 1885 and a British one – in *The Times*, no less – in 1954.

Broker

As a verb, in the sense of 'to broker a deal', 'to act as a broker, to negotiate', this feels like another vile piece of modern jargon of the 'any noun can be verbed' variety (see **ACTION**). In fact, it is first recorded in 1638. However, in the nineteenth century and for most of the twentieth its use was almost exclusively American; indeed, the 2008 *Chambers Dictionary* maintains that it still is. So this is a verb that originated in the UK, crossed the Atlantic, fell into disuse in its home country and has only recently crossed back again. Perhaps the British purists have something to complain about after all. There can be no objection to the word as a noun but, according to *Chambers*, a British broker's occupation is not *to broker* but *to broke*. And, as we all know, **IF IT AIN'T BROKE, DON'T FIX IT.**

Bottom-up

See **TOP-DOWN MANAGEMENT**.

Buying into

These days, buying into something doesn't necessarily involve parting with money. Yes, you can 'buy into' a company by investing in stocks and shares, but you can also 'buy into' a management ethos or a government policy without putting your hands in your pockets. All you are required to do is to believe them wholeheartedly and embrace them without reservation. Which, of course, may be more difficult than forking out mere cash.

Core competencies

'What we're good at, the main purpose of our business.' Businessdictionary.com has a fifty-word definition that includes 'Core competencies are what give a firm one or more competitive advantages, in creating and delivering value to its customers in its chosen field.' But 'what we're good at' sums it up.

From the same source comes the definition of 'core rigidities', the 'flip side' of core competencies: '... caused by over-reliance on any advantage(s) for too long. While a successful firm's management relaxes its improvement efforts, others keep on getting better and obsolete its competitive advantage.'

I quote that largely because I have never seen 'obsolete' used as a verb before and I hope I never do again.

Delayering

In use since at least the 1990s, this is a specific form of **DOWNSIZING** that involves disposing of tiers of management and simplifying the hierarchy. Delayering makes the organization less bureaucratic and the decision-making process quicker and thus gives the company a better competitive 'edge'. Sounds good, doesn't it? Maybe, but it is still a euphemism for people losing their jobs.

Delivery

Postmen used to deliver things (oh, those were the days). Or, if you have a really long memory, boys on bikes with baskets on the front. The delivery was therefore the post or the couple of pounds of stewing steak that you had ordered from the butcher's. Or whatever. The point is that it was a physical object. Nowadays, delivery is the means by which a service meets the **END USER**: an 'electronic delivery strategy' is jargonista speak for a plan for making services available online, while the UK Secretary of State for Culture and Related Stuff recently asserted that he would try to minimize the effect of spending cuts on 'practitioners such as writers who deliver culture on the **FRONT LINE**'. Is there a writer in the world who didn't wince on reading that?

However, it would be wrong to poke too much fun at this usage: it's a prime example of the way a common or garden word evolves to cope with a new invention or phenomenon. When the butcher's boy cycled up to the kitchen door and handed over a parcel of meat, he was, in the low-tech way appropriate to the cosy black-and-white films in which he appeared, delivering to the end user.

Direct report

Why do people think that saying things in plain English makes them look unsophisticated? Yes, this is infinitesimally quicker than saying 'someone in my department' or 'someone who reports to me', but isn't it ugly? The sense of 'report' meaning a person reporting rather than a written or verbal account has not, at the time of writing, made it into the dictionaries. And long may that continue to be the case.

Dynamic

As an adjective meaning 'energetic', this word has been around since the middle of the nineteenth century, having evolved from the science of *dynamics*, which studies movement. As a noun meaning 'an energizing force' it soon drifted away from the scientific world, so that by the late twentieth century it had come to mean first something that drove a social change ('the dynamic behind the swing to the left') then the change itself ('the new left-wing dynamic').

From there it was but a short step to management-consultant speak for 'how people get on', 'how things work': 'His not being there changed the whole dynamic of the meeting'; 'Having a few young people around changes the dynamic of the office'. This sense has yet to appear in the dictionaries, but it can't be far off.

◆

Empowerment

What is it about this word that makes the flesh creep? It's a perfectly reasonable concept, 'the action of empowering; the state of being empowered' and to empower simply means 'to give somebody power for a purpose, to enable them to do something'. Both words have been around for a hundred (in the case of empower, several hundred) years. But the modern definition of 'giving people power to take decisions about themselves, particularly with regard to self-development' belongs with all those fey courses that teach women in particular to say 'challenge' when they mean 'problem' and encourage 'personal growth and reclaiming the goddess within'.

Bill Gates has spoken about empowering workers in order to make their jobs more interesting, which will in turn make them work more diligently and enthusiastically. But he was talking about giving them information that was 'just a few clicks away' – in other words, keeping them (**IN THE) LOOP**. I don't *think* he meant that the staff of Microsoft should reclaim the goddess within, though you never know …

Engagement

This is a word that has had many shades of meaning in its time, all to do with agreements, arrangements or obligations: you might be engaged to be married or engaged to have dinner with someone next Tuesday (and have written the latter down in your engagement diary, though with luck you will have remembered the former without having to make a note of it). Two swords might be engaged in the course of a fencing match or a craftsman engaged in a delicate piece of work. Nowadays, sales and marketing people are urged to engage with their customers in order to build stronger and more profitable relationships, to ensure **BRAND** loyalty and **DELIVER** great experiences across the whole 'customer life-cycle'. It's another form of **CUSTOMER VALUE ORIENTATION** and similarly a posh name for a fairly basic concept.

Face time

Another instance of 'my time is so important, I must save every possible fraction of a second by speaking in abbreviations that have become too short to make any sense' (see **DIRECT REPORT**). Try this exercise. If your watch is sensitive enough, time yourself saying 'face time'. Then time yourself saying 'face-to-face time' (which is what it means) and calculate the difference. Now work out how many messages you could send on your Blackberry in the time you have saved. Not all that many, is my guess.

Anyway, 'face-to-face time' means 'getting together in the same room', as opposed to communicating by phone, email or whatever. We used to call it a meeting.

Facilitator

'To facilitate' is to make something easy or easier, and it has meant that since the sixteenth century. A person who facilitates has been a facilitator since the eighteenth. The beginnings of the meaning that many of us would dismiss as modern jargon – a person or organization that promotes communication or negotiation between various others, a conference organizer or co-ordinator – have been around since 1928. But as a fancy word for 'guide', someone to show you round a museum, for example, it dates, as so many expressions in this book do, from that jargon-ridden decade, the 1980s.

Functional flexibility

Isn't this a beautiful expression? To do with teamwork and being able to cover when someone else is away or when one department is more stressed than another, it translates into day-to-day English as 'being able to do lots of jobs'.

Going forward

'We'll be looking at how we can improve things going forward,' said a British Airports Authority spokesman when Heathrow was in chaos after heavy snow in the run-up to some Christmas or other (it's difficult to keep track now that this seems to be a regular feature of the run-up to Christmas). The expression means little more than 'in the future', 'from now on', with the occasional suggestion of '(**LET'S) DRAW A LINE UNDER IT**'. To all intents and purposes it's a verbal filler that could, um, be dispensed with, y'know?

Horizontal initiative

Despite what you might think at first glance, this is no more connected with sex than **MISSIONARY SELLING**. Social commentators have been making the distinction between 'horizontal' and 'vertical' (usually in terms of class or wealth) for a surprisingly long time. The Russian-born American sociologist Pitirim Sorokin was writing about horizontal and vertical social mobility as early as 1927. So it is really the use of 'initiative' that turns this expression into jargon: as an alternative to 'project' or 'idea', it has not yet been recognized by standard dictionaries, though it is in common use among lovers of gobbledygook and claptrap.

In the workplace, anything 'vertical' operates in the traditional direction of a manager telling a subordinate what to do and the subordinate doing it and reporting back. Working 'horizontally' means involving more than one department/agency/organization. This inevitably brings with it all the problems of liaising with others who are on an equal footing, so no one person is in charge; motivating people who are not answerable to you and may not feel the task is as important as you do; ensuring that, although it is a joint enterprise, you get the credit if it goes well; and making sure that your horizontal partners share the blame if it is a disaster. To counterbalance these negative aspects, in a horizontal initiative you get to use other people's data and expertise – provided, of course, they can be persuaded to share it with you.

Open-door management

Having a policy of 'Come on in, my door is always open' is supposed to encourage trust within a company; employees believe that the boss is part of the team and that any contributions they make will be taken seriously. However, management consultants are quick to point out that, for a manager, sitting in your office all day, even with the door open, is no substitute for getting out there among the workers and picking up a feel for what is going on before complaints or anxieties start to fester (see **MBWA**). Similarly, it is a foolish manager who believes that all is well, just because he has had a one-to-one meeting with a subordinate who had no issues to raise. This is much more likely to mean that his subordinates don't trust him enough to confide in him. Or that he has shot their ideas down in flames once too often and they are resigned to doing it his way, however wrong-headed they may think him. Face it, if you are the boss: you wouldn't be being paid so generously if it were easy.

Outsourcing

… is a glorified form of subcontracting. Although it can refer to goods, it is more frequently used of buying in services from another company. Outsourcing came to prominence in the 1980s, when companies were **DOWNSIZING** their permanent staff and needed freelancers to do the work on an as-and-when basis; it has since been much adopted by the public sector. Indeed, outsourcing has become such a contributor to public services that one UK-based 'services and outsourcing' company – which runs, among other things, sundry public transport services, four prisons and a major laboratory – has a turnover of almost £4 billion. To put that into perspective, there are around 40 countries in the world with lower GDPs. We're talking big business here.

Ownership

Well, obviously, we know what this means. But in the jargon context one can have 'ownership' of something as large and unownable as the environment: it's the modern term for feeling involved and taking responsibility. In the workplace, it's about taking pride in your work or wanting the company that pays your salary to do well. American business expert Michael Bergdahl wrote of Sam Walton, founder of Wal-Mart, that he 'instilled ownership of the products in the stores into the collective consciousness of every associate, regardless of what job they did for the company'. Looking at the size Wal-Mart is today, you'd have to think that it worked.

Performance coaching

We used to have management training, a wide-reaching concept whose aim was to make people better at their job. Now we have performance coaching, whose aim is fundamentally the same. Perhaps the first half of 'management training' sounded too elitist and the second too prescriptive: in the twenty-first century we are more into personal development and **EMPOWERMENT** than into telling people what to do.

Proactive

'Tending to initiate change rather than reacting to events'; in other words a **SELF-STARTER**, someone who can come up with ideas without waiting for someone else to tell them what to do.

The word has its origins in psychology and psychiatry, where it is first recorded in the 1930s. It had moved into more general parlance by the 1960s and been co-opted by business speak by the 1980s. To give an example of its use, the book *Behaviour for Learning* by Simon Ellis and Janet Tod, published in 2009, has as its subtitle 'Proactive Approaches to Behaviour Management'. Aimed at teachers, it offers 'a clear conceptual framework for making sense of the many behaviour

management strategies on offer, allowing them to make a critical assessment about their appropriateness and effectiveness in the classroom'. You might translate this as 'how to make the little blighters behave long enough to actually learn something'. The proactive part comes when you do unto them before they do unto you.

Quality-driven

See **RESULTS-DRIVEN**.

Rationalizing

The most recent definition of 'to rationalize', and the one that is relevant to us, is 'to organize (an industry) so as to achieve greater efficiency and economy'. That is *The Chambers Dictionary* at its elegant best: it carefully makes no mention of sacking people, although that is implicit.

Since the seventeenth century 'to rationalize' has meant 'to explain, to make reasonable', and since the eighteenth Rationalism has been a theological concept that helps to explain (or explain away) God. In the early twentieth century psychologists started using 'rationalizing' to describe the way patients justified their *un*reasonable behaviour, to themselves and others, with what the *OED* winningly describes as 'plausible but specious reasons'.

It was about that time – the 1920s – that economists adopted the term to describe the reorganization of a business in order to avoid wastage of time, labour or materials. As early as this (it was the decade of the General Strike – they knew all about industrial conflict) it implied specifically making cuts, reducing numbers of employees or closing down parts of a business in order to make the rest run more efficiently. In those early days, though, you rationalized a business, a department, a system; nowadays the concept is so clearly understood that the verb can be used intransitively: if you say, 'They are rationalizing in Washington', no one is going to ask, 'Rationalizing what?' or assume that the Pentagon is planning to introduce Rationalist principles.

Resource allocation

A fancy-schmancy expression for 'how you spend your money'. There are systems and matrixes and models to help you do it, but that is what it boils down to.

Results-driven

It has long been an axiom among journalists of the better sort that the way to test if an expression is a tautology or a nonsense is to consider its opposite: thus, for example, the fact that you can't have a dangerous haven or a wonderful disaster makes a mockery of 'safe haven' or 'terrible disaster'. In the same spirit, in their splendid book *Why Business People Speak Like Idiots: a bullfighter's guide* (2005), Brian Fugere, Chelsea Hardaway and Jon Warshawsky give the opposite of 'results-driven' as 'for the sheer hell of it'. They point out that, as so few business proposals have succeeded with 'for the sheer hell of it' as their declared motivation, 'results-driven' is a good expression to drop from your vocabulary.

By the same token, describing your business as 'quality-driven' becomes valid only if your competitors have come out and admitted that they deliberately produce tat. This brings you into Reggie Perrin territory, which may be an enjoyable place to be but won't do anything for the clarity of your communications.

Revenue stream

This is an expression with a wide variety of uses, all of them to a greater or lesser extent pretentious. Dating – surprisingly for something that sounds so obviously like modern jargon – from the 1920s, it can be used in the stock market, where assets may be said to have 'a future revenue stream' – that is, we can sell 'em later and make money. Governments have used 'revenue stream' because it sounds better than 'income generated by taxes'; in business it means little more than 'sales'.

Increasingly, however, it has come to mean 'a new and exciting source of income' – the Kindle is a new revenue stream for Amazon, for example, or podcasting may be a revenue stream for a radio station or newspaper. As long as the cash keeps flowing in, though, it doesn't much matter what you call it.

Skill set

This is a neologism for 'things you can do' or, as *Chambers* less perfunctorily puts it, 'a range of job-related aptitudes'. The important part of this is really the 'set': some of the attributes of an accomplished diplomat, for example, might be linguistic ability, tact, shrewdness and an awareness of the differences between various cultures. Put them all together and you have a skill set. See also **KNOWLEDGE BASE**.

Stakeholders

The earliest (eighteenth-century) stakeholders were there to see fair play in betting games, but the 'modern' sense of 'someone with a financial or other interest in the success of an organization' is almost as old: it is recorded in the 1820s. Nevertheless, it has the stigma of recent jargon about it, enabling the writers of reports to produce statements such as:

> The business models set out below take into account the stakeholders involved and our understanding of their needs and priorities ... The interests of the various stakeholders are not always well aligned, meaning that there may need to be winners and losers to make some of these business models viable.

In this context, the word means little more than 'people involved' and is one of those obfuscating terms employed by those who have a rooted objection to the use of plain English.

Then there is that mysterious entity, the stakeholder pension. A government website helpfully explains to the bemused punter that 'stakeholder pensions are a type of personal pension' and that 'stakeholder pensions work in much the same way as other money purchase pensions'. Obfuscation gone mad.

SWOT analysis

SWOT stands for 'strengths, weaknesses, opportunities and threats' and a SWOT analysis is a game played in conference rooms up and down the land when the person in charge of stationery has accidentally ordered ten years' worth of Post-it notes and they need to be used up in order to make room for other stuff in the cupboard. The idea is that a group of you gets together to consider your business, your competitors and the state of the market. You need four whiteboards or flip-charts (labelled S, W, O and T) and a supply of Post-it notes. Each person writes down any strengths, weaknesses, opportunities and threats they can think of, each on a separate Post-it. These are then stuck to the relevant board and you all gather round to read each other's contributions. With any luck, before this has palled it will be time to take the cling film

off the trays of sandwiches thoughtfully provided by the marketing manager. Once you've eaten those, it should be time to go back to work. If not, you may be able to fit in a quick round of Pin the Tail on the Donkey.

American management consultant Albert Humphrey is said to have invented SWOT analysis in the 1960s. It was initially called SOFT analysis, with the f standing for 'fault'. 'Swot' in the sense of 'someone who works hard in a nerdy sort of way' isn't commonly used in American English, so the people who made the change may have been under the mistaken impression that they were getting rid of an acronym that invited mockery.

Top-down management

Given that this means 'management telling underlings what to do', you may think that this is just the way life is and wonder if we need a term for it.

Well, apparently so, because top-down management is not as popular as it used to be. Except, it seems, when it is crucial to get things done. The rest of the time, when presumably it doesn't matter whether things get done or not, 'team-based management' is the in thing. This is defined as 'an approach that **PROACTIVELY** seeks the input of multiple **STAKEHOLDERS** in the decision-making process', which seems to combine all the best elements of muddling along and saying, 'Well, gee, I'm not sure. What do you think?' Otherwise known as 'engaging multiple perspectives within the company'.

Team-based management may also take a 'bottom-up' approach, which means it will listen to ideas from the lower echelons. This expression is not intended as an alternative to 'Cheers' when raising a glass. And see **HORIZONTAL INITIATIVE** for something else that isn't as interesting as it sounds.

Transparency

This word became a big deal in British politics at the time of the MPs' expenses scandal of 2009; the 2010 general election was full of promises of 'transparency' in order to restore the British public's faith in its representatives. Hmm.

However, 'transparency' as a guard against corruption is not a new concept. Transparency International, the self-styled 'global coalition against corruption', has for fifteen years been preparing an annual Corruption Perceptions Index which measures the perceived corruption of 178 nations on a scale of 0 (unbelievably corrupt) to 10 (equally unbelievably squeaky clean). Somalia, Afghanistan and Myanmar were 2010's lowest scorers, which is a sad reflection on the state of the world and makes the British MP who asked the public purse to pay for the cleaning of his moat look pretty pathetic.

As a matter of interest, the only countries scoring 9 or more ('practically perfect in every way') were Denmark, New Zealand and Singapore (all on 9.3) and Finland and Sweden (both 9.2). Canada was sixth with 8.9, Australia eighth with 8.7, the UK twentieth with 7.6 and the US twenty-second equal with Belgium with 7.1. It may distress those Brits who lost money when the Icelandic banks collapsed to know that

Iceland managed to beat us by a clear 0.5, to sneak into eleventh place. They must have fewer moats in Iceland. It's the only explanation.

Unconscious incompetence

This sounds as if it should be the worst possible form of incompetence: not only are you rubbish at something, you aren't even aware that you are rubbish at it. In fact this is the first stage of what is often called a **LEARNING CURVE**: you don't know how to do something but it looks easy, so you assume you could do it if you tried. You watch someone typing and are impressed by their speed. How hard can it be? You try it and realise that you are all fingers and thumbs. You have progressed to stage two: 'conscious incompetence'. Stage three, you take lessons and learn how to position your fingers; you practise and make sure that you always use your right thumb for the space bar: this is 'conscious competence' – you are aware that you are getting the hang of it. Finally, you rattle away at the keyboard just as quickly and accurately as the person who once made it look easy and you no longer have to think about it: you have reached the level of 'unconscious competence'. Or smugness, as those less proficient might call it.

(The) way forward

This is politician speak for 'the best thing to do', but somehow it sounds more positive and gives the impression that the speaker has given the matter some thought. Hearers are invited (by me, not necessarily by the politicians) to draw their own conclusions.

Window of opportunity

The point of a *window* of opportunity is that it occupies a small, limited area or time frame and should be grasped quickly; otherwise it will slip away. An early (1980) example refers to the US/USSR arms race, when the Soviets had a 'window of opportunity' to knock out some American missiles: they didn't react quickly enough and the moment passed.

From this confrontational beginning, the expression was taken up by proponents of **EMPOWERMENT** and became an inspirational cliché – meaning little more than 'opportunity' – in contexts such as, 'Life's ups and downs provide windows of opportunity to determine what is important to you. Think of them as stepping stones that will help you reach your goals.'

In the modern workplace, however, a window of opportunity (or just a window) has come to be a synonym for 'a space in my diary'. It is used by people who think they are busier and more important than you are, but you would probably be well-advised to smother your irritation and arrange a meeting (or 'set up some **FACE TIME**') with them while you have the chance.

6

KSF in FMCG

ABBREVIATIONS AND ACRONYMS

TLAs – three-letter acronyms – are all the rage in the business world, although this chapter also contains three of four letters, one of six and even one of seven. This is all very well when they are genuine acronyms: that is, they make a word you can pronounce. But some of the abbreviations are so cumbersome that you wonder why we bother. The prime example of this was WWW, which took a lot longer to say than 'worldwide web' and as a result has largely been ditched in favour of the less tongue-twisting 'web'. MBWA is almost as bad, but at least we can be reasonably certain that it was coined with a tongue in a cheek.

B2B

Even those who rail against everything possible being abbreviated these days will admit that 'business to business' is a bit of a mouthful after a decent lunch. They'd also find it hard to deny that, although the introduction of the figure 2 is both inaccurate and meaningless, BtoB would have been a rubbish acronym.

The point about B2B is that it involves two businesses, rather than a business and a consumer, as this 1998 quote from the *Financial Times* makes clear: 'These potential **REVENUE STREAMS** present growth opportunities for incumbents and a fresh **PARADIGM** for new entrants, both of which feel compelled to embrace B2B (business-to-business) in order to succeed.' When I say 'clear', I mean, of course, '... as mud'.

BCP/BPCP

See **DRP**.

BOGOF

A prime example of the power of **PULL MARKETING**, this is an ugly-sounding acronym for what most people think of as an attractive concept – 'buy one, get one free'. **BOGOHP** ('...get one half price') is another familiar ploy, but for some reason hasn't passed into the language as an acronym. The abbreviation BOGOF has been around for a quarter of a century, but has been used with increasing frequency in recent years as retailers have become more and more desperate for our custom. It's now not unusual to see it spelt bogof, without explanation or inverted commas – so that, as with radar and scuba, we'll soon be forgetting that it was ever an acronym at all.

CBD

'Central business district' is self-explanatory and it's a term that has been with us since at least 1960. I include it only as an excuse to quote the Yorkshire poet Ian McMillan on the subject of his hometown of Darfield (population at the last census 8,066). In an article in the *Yorkshire Post* in 2009 he described a bus ride that rambled round the houses on its way to 'Darfield's Central Business District, as we call Mad Geoff's the Barber's, the Co-op Chemist, the Paper Shop and the Supermarket'. Darfield's out-of-town shopping centre must be very dull by comparison.

DRP

This concept is probably best defined by the subtitle of the bible on the subject, *Disaster Recovery Planning*, by American IT consultant Jon William Toigo: it is 'Preparing for the Unthinkable'.

The point of DRP – also known as BCP or BPCP (business continuity plan or business process contingency plan) – is that if you plan ahead thoroughly enough, you will be prepared even if the absolute worst happens. The effects of a disaster will be minimized and normal service will be resumed as soon as possible. As IT systems become ever more complex, of course, there are more and more things that can go wrong and, in order to be of any use at all, disaster recovery plans have to be ever more sophisticated. Standing in the car park drying circuit boards with a hair dryer just doesn't cut it any more.

Mr Toigo has been preaching his message for twenty years, but his Disaster Recovery site reports limited **PENETRATION**: 'Despite the number of very public disasters since 9/11, still only about 50 per cent of companies report having a disaster recovery plan. Of those that do, nearly half have never tested their plan, which is tantamount to not having one at all.' A worrying thought, suggesting that too many of us are relying on **FIRE-FIGHTING**.

ETA

An extraordinarily versatile – some might say dangerously ambiguous – abbreviation whose meaning depends entirely on where and who you are and what you are doing. If you're travelling, it could be either Estimated Time of Arrival

(an expression that dates back to the Second World War) or Electronic Travel Authority, an alternative to a visa for entry into Australia (rather more recent). If you're in charge of an oil tanker, it is likely to be Emergency Towing Arrangement. In the IT world, it could be Embedded Transport Acceleration, developed by Intel with a view to speeding up communication between servers. A stargazer may translate it as Extraterrestrial Activity; for a Basque separatist it is the name of a political party, although in Spanish it is also an abbreviation for Automated Weather Stations. In Portugal it is short for 'I love you'.

In other words, be careful how you use it. Particularly in Portugal.

FMCG

The website www.fmcg.co.uk (yes, there really is such a thing) defines fast-moving consumer goods as 'simply the essential items that one must have in order to live – or at least live well'. The most obvious FMCGs are items that leave the supermarket shelves quickly, things that most people buy most weeks. However, you don't have to go to the supermarket to buy FMCGs: they can be delivered to your home, or they can include something you might pick up from a market stall, a pharmacy or a 'tobacco or smoking paraphernalia store'. Stationery, confectionery and booze are also FMCGs and, if you are willing to stretch the definition a little further, you can include MP3 players, iPods and the like, which are changed frequently in order to keep up with the latest trends.

The point of fast-moving consumer goods is, from the customer's point of view, that they are cheap and have a short life-expectancy; as far as manufacturers and retailers are concerned, margins may be low but the goods sell in sufficiently high volume for the overall profit to be substantial. The opposite of an FMCG is a consumer durable, such as a washing machine, which is more expensive, lasts longer, is bought in smaller quantities but has a higher profit margin on each item. It isn't usually referred to as a CD, for the simple reason that the inventors of compact discs got there first.

FPO

See **IPO**.

FUD

Fear, uncertainty and doubt are three closely related negative feelings deliberately planted in the minds of the public by those involved in marketing, PR, politics and other **SPIN**-related disciplines. FUD-spreaders tend to belong to the big companies, the major parties, the mainstream generally; their aim is to make their customers or voters scared to buy a new product and vote for an unproven party. Computing entrepreneur Gene Amdahl left IBM to set up the company that bears his name in the 1970s and accused his former employer of instilling FUD in the minds of potential customers for Amdahl products. He may have invented – and he certainly popularized – the acronym, but the concept had been around for at least half a century before he used it.

Opponents of FUD have used terms such as 'implicit coercion' and 'disinformation' with reference to computer giants and others; they have also found themselves in court as a result, so let's leave it there.

If by any chance you pursue wildfowl shooting as a hobby, particularly in Australia, you may think that FUD stands for 'fold-up decoy'– a flat-pack version of a decoy used in pursuit of ducks, geese and pigeons. If so, I'm afraid you may somehow have strayed into the wrong book.

IPO

An initial public offering is the first offering of stock for sale to the public by a private company. According to the website investopedia.com, IPOs are often issued by small companies seeking the capital to expand, but sometimes also by large privately owned companies looking to become publicly traded. The site goes on to advise that ...

> ... IPOs can be a risky investment. For the individual investor, it is tough to predict what the stock will do on its initial day of trading and in the near future because there is often little historical data with which to analyse the company. Also, most IPOs are of companies going through a transitory growth period, which are subject to additional uncertainty regarding their future values.

So, if you're looking for a secure investment, it may be prudent to wait for an FPO (Follow-on Public Offering), a supplementary issue of shares made once a company is established on a stock exchange.

KPI

Key performance indicators must be measurable (there's a lot of that about in business speak: see **DASHBOARD**). And – clue in the title – they have to be *key* to a organization's performance. As one management website puts it, 'Once an organization has analysed its **MISSION** and defined its goals, it needs a way to measure progress towards those goals. Key Performance Indicators are these measurements.' Goals can be nebulous; KPIs can't. So a goal could be 'to be the most popular company in our field', but a KPI would have to be something like 'percentage of first-time customers coming back for more'.

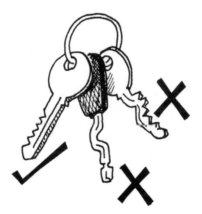

What form KPIs take obviously depends on the nature of your business. If you are running a bus company, for example, one indicator might be the percentage of buses that arrive on time; if you are in a customer-service department, it might be the percentage of calls answered within five rings. Handy hint: if it's got a number in it, it's got a fighting chance of being a KPI; if not, it is more likely to be a goal or a mission or one of the three wishes that the genie granted you.

KSFs

'Key success factors': in marketing speak, the factors (they are almost always plural) that are necessary for a company to succeed in a given market. If you know the two or three things that you absolutely have to be good at, and are good at them, you can get away with being mediocre in everything else. A comforting thought for the mediocrities among us.

MBWA

Management consultants Tom Peters and Robert H Waterman Jr made the concept of 'management by wandering around' famous in their 1982 book *In Search of Excellence*, reckoned by those in the know to be one of the best business books of the century. The idea was to make senior management visible and available to employees, to show that the boss was interested in how everyone was getting on and was responsive to any suggestions they had to make. One website – not connected with Messrs Peters or Waterman – offers ten top tips to assist the would-be MBWAer, but rather spoils the effect by including 'Make certain your visits are spontaneous and unplanned.' See also the less **PROACTIVE** but still well-intentioned **OPEN-DOOR MANAGEMENT.**

OEM

There are some strange acronyms and abbreviations around in the modern world, but this is one of the strangest: how, you may well ask, did OEM come to stand for 'intermediate user'?

It started out sensibly enough, as an abbreviation for Original Equipment Manufacturer. An Original Equipment Manufacturer manufactures a product. A washing machine, say. So far so good. Then the OEM sells that washing machine to a retailer to be sold under its 'own brand' label. The retailer makes money, the customer has clean clothes, everyone is happy.

But let's imagine that the product isn't something finished, like a washing machine, but a computer component. The company that purchases it from the OEM isn't the retailer but an intermediary whose task is to incorporate the component into the finished item and *then* sell it on. From the retailer's point of view, it's all the same thing – he's buying a product and is doesn't matter whether the supplier is the originator or not. So that intermediary also becomes an OEM, to simplify the coding on the retailer's paperwork. As far as the intermediary is concerned, the retailer is the customer, the customer is always right, so logic goes out the window and an

OEM becomes an intermediate user. QED, some might say. And see also **VAR**.

RBM

Results-based management has been defined as 'a management strategy by which an organization ensures that its processes, products and services contribute to the achievement of desired results (outputs, outcomes and impacts)'. The planning process which is integral to this form of management 'starts with defining objectives – deciding what accomplishments are expected if the objective is to be achieved, determining which output will lead to those accomplishments, defining the activities necessary to produce those outputs and, finally, identifying the inputs that are necessary to carry out the activities'.

It all sounds very sensible, if a bit long-winded, but it makes you wonder what the opposite is: MIUAWGAASWH? That stands for 'making it up as we go along and seeing what happens' and I can see that it isn't as snappy-sounding as it needs to be. Perhaps that's why it hasn't caught on with the jargonistas. See also **RESULTS-DRIVEN**.

SMB

Do we need a formal abbreviation for 'small and medium-sized businesses'? Apparently so, though if we prefer not to confuse them with the San Miguel Beermen (a Filipino basketball team), a System Management Bus, a Server Message Block (both computing terms too complicated to go into here) or the Spartan Marching Band of Michigan State University, we can call them SMEs ('small and medium-sized enterprises') instead. However, we then run the risk of confusing them with the Society of Manufacturing Engineers, a NASA satellite called the Solar Mesosphere Explorer and an economic model known as Social Market Economy. A bit like ETA, these are abbreviations that need to be used with care. The issue is also complicated by the fact that different countries define 'small' and 'medium' in different ways: what is considered small in Canada (fewer than a hundred employees in some industries) would be quite a decent size in New Zealand, for example. But then if you look at a map you can imagine that the same would be true of a number of things in those two countries.

Anyway, many governments, and multinational organizations such as the European Commission, give state aid, grants for research and development, etc. to small and medium-sized businesses, so they have to be able to define them. And, having just typed small and medium-sized businesses/enterprises a number of times in the space of this entry, I can see why they decided it did indeed need to be abbreviated.

USP

Meaning 'unique selling point' or 'unique selling proposition', this has been the mantra of anyone involved in marketing since 1958. The three rules for a USP were defined in that year

by advertising guru Rosser Reeves, the man who came up with the line 'Melts in your mouth, not in your hands' to sell M & Ms. 'First,' he said, 'you need a definite proposition. Then, second, it must be a unique proposition. Third, the proposition must sell.' Like so many ideas with which we have all grown up, it seems obvious now, but it was revolutionary at the time.

VAR

Short for value-added reseller, this refers to a company, probably in the computer world, that buys in a product from another company, adds 'value' to it, perhaps by introducing its own software, and moves it on at a higher price. If what is being supplied is a service rather than a product, it may be described as a VAS (whose meaning you can probably work out for yourself). This may, for example, enable users of mobile phones to log on to the internet, play video games and do all sorts of other things over and above making phone calls. 'Value added' is frequently used on its own as a noun, to indicate 'the amount of value that is added' at each stage of an item's production. It could have been called 'added value', but that wouldn't have won it a place in the economics jargon stakes.

As a matter of interest, the concept of value-added tax – surely an all-too-transparent euphemism for 'price-added tax' – was proposed in Germany in 1918, though the first people to introduce it on a large scale were the French, in 1954. It came to the UK in the early '70s, as part of a BUNDLE of benefits of joining the European Community.

WOMBAT

An acronym born of the 'get it all into 140 characters' culture, this is variously translated as 'waste of money, brains and time' or '... and talent'. Whether or not it stands the test of time remains to be seen but, like many such coinages, it is kind of cute.

WYSIWYG

'What you see is what you get'. Originally (in the 1980s) this meant that what you saw on your computer screen was exactly what you would get on a print-out: an important concept in the days when the difference between screen fonts and printer fonts caused many a nightmare for those involved in graphic design. Tending to fall into disuse in its original sense, the longer form of this acronym is sometimes used as a set phrase in a social context: someone who doesn't bother to dress up for formal occasions or isn't renowned for the polish of his manners might, with a sense of inverted snobbery, describe himself as a 'what-you-see-is-what-you-get sort of guy'. If you are the host, you are under no obligation to invite this person again.

7

Creative accounting

MONEY, ITS USES AND ABUSES

When all is said and done, it's a business. People are in it for the money. Not all of them are dishonest, but just as somebody once wondered why the devil should have all the best tunes, so you might similarly ask why the swindlers have the most imaginative turns of phrase.

Anti-trust

This makes sense only if you are aware of a specific definition of trust: 'a group of commercial enterprises combined to monopolize and control the market for any commodity: illegal in the US'. Thus in America there are anti-trust laws which prohibit the sort of thing that in the UK would be referred to the Competition Commission or, in the past, to the Monopolies and Mergers Commission.

Anti-trust legislation has been around for over a hundred years, but when the economy went global the expression started to crop up in the British news and, until we became accustomed to it, appeared strange to those of us brought up to think that trust was a good thing.

Asset-purchasing

See **QUANTITATIVE EASING**.

Asset-stripping

With no ancestry other than in the business world, this expression emerged in the 1970s to describe the action of flogging off bits of a company you had just taken over in order to make a quick profit. The implication is that you – the purchaser – were after only one thing, which in this instance wasn't sex. Say, for example, you bought the Louvre because you longed to own the Mona Lisa, and then dispersed all the Botticellis and Titians to the highest bidder: there aren't many people in the art world who wouldn't call you a Philistine. Though of course with all that money and your favourite painting over the fireplace you might not care a great deal.

Ballpark

A ballpark used to be a stadium where baseball was played. It probably still is. Then, during the Second World War, it came to mean any area roughly the size of a ballpark; later, in the early years of space exploration, it was specifically the area within which the capsule from a satellite returning to Earth was supposed to land.

Next it evolved the figurative sense of any general area, so that a financial offer might not be quite as much as the vendor wanted but was 'in the right ballpark' – that is, not ludicrously low; with a bit of negotiation a deal was likely to be struck. From this use, it developed into today's adjective, so that we have 'a ballpark figure' (not unlike a 'back of the envelope figure'), meaning 'an educated guess, something to work with while waiting for someone to do the sums properly'. First recorded in 1960, a ballpark figure is a newer concept than a GUESSTIMATE, but not necessarily a more accurate one.

As a noun, a ballpark can also be 'an area of expertise', as in 'I am not qualified to express an opinion; this is not my ballpark' – though if you chose to learn more about that sphere of activity you could find yourself in a whole new ballgame.

Black-box accounting

The term 'black box' – which to most of us means the thing that helps experts find out why an aeroplane has crashed – is used in computing and engineering to mean a self-contained unit whose workings need not be understood by the user. In the accounting world, it is more or less synonymous with a 'dark hole' – a place into which numbers vanish without trace or from which they appear as if by magic.

This concept entered public awareness at the time of the Enron scandal in 2001 and is defined (by investorwords.com) as 'complex and confusing accounting METHODOLOGY that makes financial statements hard to interpret by an untrained individual'. Enron used it to manipulate its share price and disguise the fact that the company had no assets. Shareholders

eventually lost some $11 billion and a number of those responsible went to jail. If the **CREATIVE ACCOUNTING** used in *The Producers* rendered the offenders 'incredibly guilty', what was happening at Enron really does beggar belief.

Black Friday

In the UK a 'black' day is traditionally one on which disaster strikes in the City. There was a Black Monday in October 1987 when stock markets around the world crashed; and a Black Wednesday in September 1992 when the UK withdrew from the European Exchange Rate Mechanism because of the weakness of the pound. Politically incorrect it may be, but in this context black = bad.

In the US, however, the 'black' of Black Friday means 'going into the black': it refers to the day after Thanksgiving (which falls on the fourth Thursday of November), when lots of people take an unofficial holiday. On this day Christmas shopping suddenly takes off and retailers expect their businesses to start making a profit. In the last few years the marketing people have also created Cyber Monday, the Monday following Black Friday, when massive discounts are offered to encourage people to shop online. Whether you choose to do battle with the High Street crowds or stay home in front of the computer, it's all about somebody out there finding a way to take your money.

Bottom line

This used to mean the figure at the bottom of a financial statement, indicating whether or not the company had made money. From there, from the 1960s, it expanded to cover a result or outcome of more or less any description: 'The bottom line is that they decided to get married in Vegas.' Having lost any grip on its grammatical origins, the phrase is now often used as a stand-alone to mean something like 'to cut a long story short' or 'when you get right down to it': 'So, bottom line, if the weather doesn't improve I won't make it to the airport on time.'

Cash cow

An expression that has been around since the 1970s, a cash cow is a part of a business that you can *milk* (oh yes, there is method in some of this madness) to provide a steady source of income. It also has the advantage of requiring little investment or maintenance. The danger is that you become impatient with the plodding, cud-chewing nature of your cow and, in an effort to make it produce faster profits, turn it into the goose that laid the golden egg. Which is either a horrible mixed metaphor or a dystopian vision of a future in which cloning has gone mad. Or both.

Cost driver

This is marketing speak for 'anything that effects the cost'. Cost drivers may include the cost of raw materials; economies of scale (make lots so that each individual one is cheaper); the importance of fixed versus variable costs (you can't get out of paying rent on the factory, but perhaps you can save on advertising); the number of links there are in your SUPPLY CHAIN and how much profit each needs to make, etc., etc. Understanding cost drivers is a key factor in a successful business: you don't need to be Bill Gates to see that knowing how much your product is going to cost goes a long way towards helping you work out your likely profits. After that, all you have to do is predict how many you are going to sell. See CONSUMER BACKLASH, CONSUMER CONFIDENCE and CUSTOMER VALUE ORIENTATION for factors that may have an impact there.

Creative accounting

The *OED* defines this as 'the modification of accounts to achieve a desired end; falsification of accounts that is misleading but not necessarily illegal'. It also quotes Mel Brooks's screenplay for *The Producers* (1967), in which a theatrical producer's books are comprehensively cooked so that he stands to make more money from a flop than from a hit. When, in this film, the producer is finally taken to court, the jury finds him 'incredibly guilty', suggesting that in describing the practice as 'not necessarily illegal' the *OED* takes a more lenient view than many of us might do – particularly if we were on the receiving end of it.

Dead cat bounce

An expression that arose in the stock markets of Singapore and Malaysia and was adopted by Wall Street in the mid-1980s. On the basis that 'even a dead cat will bounce if it is dropped from a great height', it is used to describe a brief upturn in the value of a particular stock or of a stock market in general, after it has hit rock bottom. But the emphasis is on the 'brief': a dead cat, having bounced, will in due course just **HIT THE GROUND** again – and it won't be running. See also **DON'T FIGHT THE TAPE** for advice on what not to do at the time of an upturn.

Done deal

This is shorthand for 'a deal that has been done', but there's something faintly defiant about it: the subtext is often 'Don't argue with me, it's too late to change it now.' Alternatively, there may be an element of subterfuge, a suggestion that, although discussions are being held, they are token and the decision has already been made. Or, a third type of nuance, someone involved is being presumptuous or premature: 'He's behaving as if it were a done deal [but it may yet fall through].' Origin? Like so many of the terms in this book, it was born in the US, late 1970s or thereabouts.

Don't fight the tape

The tape in question is the ticker tape – once paper, now electronic – used from the 1860s to transmit stock-market prices by telegraph around the world. 'Don't fight the tape' is a stockbrokers' maxim of long standing, meaning 'Don't go against the trends'. If the tape tells you the market is going up, don't bet on it going down.

Double-dip

Of a recession, this is the kind that makes a bit of a recovery, then thinks better of it and goes back into recession. Much in the news at the time of writing – and who knows where it will end?

A double-dip recession is not to be confused with the wonderful American concept of double-dipping – that is, retiring from the military, taking a pension, then accepting a 'consultancy' role with the government which in the fullness of time brings with it another pension. The reference here is not to the rollercoaster effect of a recession, but to dipping twice into an ice-cream tub to come up with two scoops. Or, to mix a metaphor, having two bites of the cherry.

Due diligence

This started out as a self-explanatory legal term, meaning the amount of care that was necessary in any given set of circumstances. From this it developed (from the 1960s, but used with increasing frequency in the last decade or so) into an appraisal of a company undertaken by or on behalf of someone considering taking it over, to assess whether or not it was a shrewd investment. So from being a description of an investigation ('X carried out the investigation into Y with due diligence') it has become the investigation itself ('X carried out a due diligence into Y'). It can be only a matter of time before the original meaning is so far forgotten that it will be possible to carry out a due diligence carelessly.

Guesstimate

Not difficult to analyse: it's a combination of a guess and an estimate. It dates back as far as the 1930s in the US and crossed the Atlantic in the 1960s. See also **BALLPARK**.

Leverage

When Archimedes said, 'Give me but one firm spot on which to stand and I shall move the earth', he was talking about leverage. With a long enough lever tucked under the South Pole at one end and enough force applied to the other, he could lift up the globe.

In this literal sense the word has been around for hundreds of years, but it acquired its figurative meaning of 'increased advantage or power' surprisingly early: future Prime Minister William Gladstone was using it in 1858. Nowadays it is (all too frequently, some would say) adopted as a jargonesque alternative to 'power', particularly 'buying power', as in 'the large chains have more leverage than the independent outlets'.

There is also a specific financial sense, in existence since the 1930s. 'To leverage' means 'to invest borrowed capital in the hope of making profits that will more than cover the interest you have to pay on the loan' and thus to gain control of something that you couldn't afford to buy if you used your own money. In the US, the expression has often been applied to a management buyout, fending off a hostile takeover bid with borrowed capital. In this instance, the person lending the money might be described as a **WHITE KNIGHT**.

Licence to print money

In the twenty-first century, most countries have a central bank that prints their only legal bank notes. These banks regulate the amount of money in circulation as a means of controlling inflation: you can't just keep printing it, apparently – it doesn't work that way.

But obviously if you *could* print your own money (and not have the taxman banging on your door and hauling you off to jail as a result) you would soon become immensely rich. Or, to turn it round the other way, if you were in possession of something immensely lucrative, you would have a meta-phorical licence to print money. Opinions vary as to when the expression was coined, as it were: it is often attributed to the press baron Lord Thomson of Fleet, with reference to his ownership of Scottish Television, a newborn commercial

channel, in the 1950s. He certainly said it, but there is evidence that it had been used in the US ten years earlier. Perhaps it is such an appealing concept that it independently tickled the fancy of more than one entrepreneur. See **QUANTITATIVE EASING** for a modern variation on the theme.

Lifecycle assessment/costing

In the old days, a lifecycle wasn't something you could assess or cost: it simply happened. The lifecycle of a butterfly, for example, was egg, caterpillar, chrysalis, butterfly, with the butterfly then laying more eggs and the process beginning again. But around the 1960s the butterfly spread its wings and moved into economics, sociology, business and, in due course, the environmental movement.

Lifecycle or whole-life costing considers not just the purchase price of an item, but what it has already cost to develop, what it will cost to keep running and, eventually, what it will cost (financially and environmentally) to dispose of. The environmental aspect has, not surprisingly, become more important in recent decades: lifecycle analysis, assessment and inventory, also known as cradle-to-the-grave analysis, are common terms in the eco-conscious part of the industrial world. They all assess the energy-consuming or pollution-producing effects of manufacturing a product, transporting it wherever it needs to go, using it until it falls apart and then burning it or carting it off to a landfill. Buy local and biodegradable is the message.

Lipstick index/lipstick indicator

An expression coined by Leonard Lauder, son of Estée and chairman of the cosmetics company that bears her name, at the time of a recession in the first years of this century. His theory was that, in a period of economic uncertainty, when a woman may feel guilty about splashing out on new shoes or a handbag, she compensates by indulging in smaller treats such as lipstick. Increased sales of lipstick, therefore, could be a sign of poor economic health. Economists don't really believe this, but then most of them are men.

Ponzi scheme

Formerly known as a bubble (from its extreme burst-ability) and made famous in recent years by the disgraced American financier Bernie Madoff, a Ponzi scheme is a scam that lures in investors by promising high and rapid returns. The problem is that there is no company making profits at the heart of the scheme: investor A receives dividends or profits from money put in by investor B, who in turn needs there to be an investor C if he is to have any return on his own capital. As long as there are enough investors it doesn't matter that there are no genuine profits, but sooner or later the whole thing tends to blow up in someone's face.

The name honours, if that is the word, an Italian-American called Charles Ponzi (1882–1949), who became a millionaire on the back of a dodgy business involving postal reply coupons (the ones that you sent instead of a stamped addressed envelope if you were dealing with someone overseas). The sums of money involved were mind-boggling and when it all fell apart no fewer than six banks collapsed as a result. Ponzi was in and out of jail for the next fifteen years and ended his life in poverty. But hey, he said in not quite so many words, it was fun while it lasted.

Quantitative easing

The Bank of England's website tells us firmly that quantitative easing is *not* a **LICENCE TO PRINT MONEY**. It's a licence to create money electronically. Not the same thing at all.

When the global financial crisis seemed to be running out of control in late 2008/early 2009, the UK's Monetary Policy Committee took action to keep the rate of inflation at the desired 2 per cent. It boosted the supply of money by purchasing assets such as government and corporate bonds, which is why the policy is also known as 'asset-purchasing' (nothing, I hasten to point out, to do with ASSET-STRIPPING). The Bank, its website tells us, 'pays for these assets by creating money electronically and crediting the accounts of the companies it bought the assets from. This extra money supports more spending in the economy to bring future inflation back to the target.'

I don't pretend to understand it, but it seems a far cry from the Gold Standard to me.

White knight

The White Knight in Lewis Carroll's *Through the Looking-Glass* (1872) means well but doesn't have much of a clue: he is constantly falling off his horse and doesn't realize that keeping a box upside down without closing the lid means everything in it will fall out. In the years following the book's publication 'white knight' came to be used for all sorts of people who fought corruption or rescued damsels in distress, although they were generally more enthusiastic than proficient. By about 1980, the term had taken on a specific meaning on the stock exchange and the suggestion of ineptitude had been lost: a white knight is someone who comes to the rescue of a company facing a hostile takeover bid. See also LEVERAGE.

At the click of a mouse

IT AND THE WEB

Since the world went electronic, all sorts of concepts that would have baffled our grandparents have become commonplace and if we are to talk about them they need to have names. This chapter can do no more than scratch the surface of the expressions that have come into being, or taken on a new lease of life, in the computer age.

Agile development

Coined in the 2001 'Manifesto for Agile Software Development', this means developing software that works, suits customer needs and can respond to change rather than rigidly following a plan. Or, as the Wikipedia entry prefers to put it, 'Agile software development is a group of software development **METHODOLOGIES** based on iterative and incremental development, where requirements and solutions evolve through collaboration between self-organizing, cross-functional teams.' While the concept seems entirely commendable, there is something about an explanation containing no fewer than five business-speak clichés in a single sentence that sticks in the craw.

(At the) click of a mouse

Once upon a time, and it seems a very long time ago now, we were exhorted to buy things that worked 'at the touch of a button'. Gone were the days of slaving over a hot mangle in order to dry clothes: the new electric washer-dryer accomplished the same task 'at the touch of a button'. All very well until the wretched thing broke down and left you – and your downstairs neighbours – ankle-deep in rapidly cooling grey water.

Now, anything you could possibly want to buy, from holidays to theatre tickets to a STATE-OF-THE-ART version of that same washer-dryer, is available 'at the click of a mouse'.

Except, of course, that it isn't. It is, at a conservative estimate, available at twenty-seven clicks of the mouse. You click to choose your own seats, click to add a hotel or a hire car or a programme or a glass of prosecco at the interval. You click to use the same credit card as you used last time and click again to have your tickets delivered to the same address as they are always delivered to – provided, of course, that that is the address to which your credit card bills are sent.

Sorry, I was just getting into this when an error occurred in the application. Please contact support. Thank you for your patience and understanding.

The *OED* defines the adjective 'one-click' as 'relating to or designating a computer operation performed with one click of a mouse button' and dates it to 1985. Ah, those were younger and simpler days.

Closure

This is a word with a long and varied pedigree: its earliest senses (a fence or barrier, or an enclosure, now obsolete) date back to the fourteenth and fifteenth centuries, and even the most literal current sense (the act of closing) is seventeenth-century. Shakespeare used it in the sense of 'bringing something to an end' and in 1882 a new law giving the British House of Commons the right to vote to close a debate brought a further refinement of the meaning. So, at a pinch, if someone scoffed at your business jargon when you were boasting about 'the closure of a deal' you could claim that you were emulating Shakespeare. At a pinch.

'Closure' has additional technical applications in phonetics and geology; and in the 1920s it was adopted by Gestalt psychologists to refer to the human tendency to see an incomplete figure such as a circle with a gap in it as more complete than it is. It is probably from this usage that we developed the originally psychoanalytical and now merely psychobabble sense of 'a feeling that an emotionally difficult experience has been dealt with and can be considered to be in the past'.

In the IT world, however, the word has gone off at a tangent of its own: in programming languages, according to wordiq.com, a closure is 'an abstraction representing a function, plus the lexical environment . . . in which the function was created, and its application to arguments. A closure results in a fully closed term: one with no free variables left.' The term was defined in the 1960s by the British computer scientist Peter Landin and I am sure we should all be very grateful.

Cloud-based

In computing terms, this means 'on a server' or 'on the Internet' and is used of software that is downloaded each time it is used, rather than being stored on a particular piece of hardware. It allows purveyors of apps, e-books and the like to offer 'anywhere, anytime' services. It may sound like what the Luddites among us call 'in the ether', but at the time of writing it is being viewed as the Next Big Thing. (Given the speed at which these things develop, that probably means it will be passé by the time this book is published, but what can you do?)

Wikipedia tells us that cloud computing has 'skyrocketed' in recent years, an odd piece of imagery which just adds to that eerie feeling of 'it's out there somewhere and Big Brother is probably watching it'.

Cyberspace

Cyber– comes from the Greek meaning 'to steer' and its earliest appearance in modern English was in *cybernetics*, the branch of science that studies control systems in mechanical and electronic devices and compares them with biological systems to see which works better. A somewhat specialist branch of science, you might think, but that's what it does. The word was coined in the 1940s, but from the 1960s *cyber–* was adopted as a prefix by science-fiction writers (a *cybernaut* was a particularly nasty sort of robot and *cyberculture* a dehumanized vision of a future society). Then the Internet came along and made the *cyber-* world its own; *cyberspace* was coined to mean 'the notional place in which Internet communication takes place'. So widespread has this become, of course, that you can now shop at *cybershops*, have *cybersex* with a person you know only online and buy a *cyberpet*, which is less likely than a guinea pig to upset the kids by dying.

Forum

Forum is the Latin for a market place, and the forum was the focal point of Roman towns throughout the Empire. The law courts were in the forum, and it was here that public speeches were made, decisions were come to and gossip of a political, commercial or personal nature was exchanged. A forum, therefore, came to mean any arena (another word borrowed directly from the Ancient Romans) where discussions were held, particularly legal ones: this is where the word 'forensic' comes from. The term gradually broadened to embrace less formal discussions which, in recent decades, could take place online, without the need for the participants to be in the same room or, as we now call it, sharing FACE TIME.

Gatekeeper

'An individual who controls the flow of information into, within or between organizations and decides who will be granted and who denied access.' People who kept the gates of cities or castles in olden times had similar powers; for the last century or more the metaphorical use has extended to those who control admission to colleges and universities, access to medical specialists and the dissemination (or not) of information to the mass media. These days gatekeepers tend not to pour boiling oil on those who seek access to whatever they control, but otherwise they can be just as strict as their medieval equivalents.

Hard-wired

If something is hard-wired into a computer it is fixed, unchangeable and cannot be modified by any software that may later be added. Shortly after the expression was invented, in the 1960s, it came to be used also of the bodily functions that are immovably associated with certain parts of the brain – memory is linked to the cerebral cortex, breathing is controlled by the medulla oblongata, etc., and there is nothing you can do about it. Thus hard-wiring comes to be associated with inflexibility: 'She was hard-wired to go home at 5.30 sharp, whether the job was finished or not.' You may feel this is to be discouraged, but the point about hard-wiring is that all the discouragement in the world won't make a blind bit of difference: it is there, and it is there to stay.

Information design

One of the more helpful concepts to emerge from the gobbledygook that surrounds IT, information design means design that is focused on conveying information. On the understanding that a picture may be worth a thousand words, it frequently uses diagrams to illustrate unfamiliar concepts – and the better designed the diagram, the more easily the ill-informed will grasp the information. Thank you, whoever invented this. It's a good thing.

Information overload

This, on the other hand, is a bad thing. Put too much information into a computer and it will crash. Throw too much information at a person and he or she will collapse under the strain. Information overload is a concept that has been around for half a century, but has become more serious since the advent of the Internet: faced with the prospect of sifting through 20,461,356 hits on Google to find the kernel of information we need, most of us would be tempted to crash. When taken to extremes, this situation can lead to information fatigue syndrome, which has, since the 1990s, been recognized (surely satirically) as a disease, but really boils down to 'Enough already!'

Input

In the sense of 'a financial contribution, something put in', this dates back to the eighteenth century. For our purposes, however, it was co-opted into the world of computing in the 1940s, to mean 'the process of feeding in data, or the data itself'. From there it spread out again to mean a contribution in the sense of an opinion: 'We can't go ahead without asking the STAKEHOLDERS for their input.' It's a perfectly pleasant, neutral word: there is no suggestion that the stakeholders are shoving their oar in where it isn't wanted (though goodness knows they do that often enough).

Knowledge base

Although this has a specialist application in computing – 'a collection of knowledge formulated for use in certain systems' – its broader meaning goes back further than that. As early as the 1950s 'knowledge base' was being used in business to mean any store of information on which decisions could be based. In those days it had a formal ring to it – the knowledge tended to be accumulated and made available in a structured manner. Nowadays it is more haphazard: an individual starting a new job may talk about 'enhancing my knowledge base' to mean little more than 'learning the details that are specific to this job as opposed to the very similar job I used to do'. In other words, in common parlance it means more than just 'knowledge' – but not much more. See also SKILL SET.

(In the) loop

In computing, a loop is a series of instructions within a program that the computer will perform over and over again until some specified condition is met; only then can it move on to its next function. In that context, 'in the loop' is first found in the 1940s. By the 1970s it had broadened to include almost any sort of information: someone unable to attend an important meeting might be briefed afterwards to keep her 'in the loop'; nowadays someone working from home can log on to the company's server to keep herself 'in the loop'. Conversely, if you don't want someone to be privy to confidential information, you can make a point of keeping her 'out of the loop'. See also (UP TO) SPEED.

Malware

This is the technical term for computer viruses and the like – programs intended to be damaging or disruptive. It feels as if it should be an ultra-modern concept, belonging to the generation of Wikileaks, but in fact the *OED*'s earliest example is dated 1990 and the concept had clearly been familiar to techies before then.

Orphan

Assuming you've seen *Oliver!*, even if you haven't read *Oliver Twist*, you probably think you know what an orphan is. But it is much more than a child who has lost its parents. The word has always been applied to a wide variety of things that have been deserted or neglected (the human race, seemingly forsaken by God, is one literary example). Then in the 1970s 'orphan' came to be used for diseases that affected so few people (or such poor people) that it was not economically viable for a drug company to research a cure. It now also refers to obsolete computer hardware and other non-biodegradable goods whose manufacturers have gone out of business and cannot take responsibility for disposing of them; to content whose copyright owners cannot be traced; and, perhaps most worryingly, to the victims of firms apparently guilty of fraud that have since managed to disappear. Like Oliver Twist, these are all things that might be considered abandoned by someone who ought to be looking after them.

Paywall

Sometimes written as two words, this is the point on a website beyond which access to content ceases to be free. Many online newspapers and academic journals allow the casual browser to read an introductory paragraph or abstract, then charge for access to the entire article. The term, comprising two self-explanatory elements, is a recent one, coined in the early years of this century when the need for it arose.

Procurement

Time was when procuring was indissolubly linked with prostitution and a procuress was what Shakespeare's dramatis personae called a bawd. Then the word acquired a military sense – the procurement division in a First or Second World War army was in charge of acquiring equipment and supplies. Come the 1980s – that decade again – you could procure in the IT world and now procurement has a broad remit, meaning 'the acquiring of the appropriate goods and services at the best possible price so that everything is in the right place at the right time'.

Straw man proposal

A modern version of **RUNNING IT UP THE FLAGPOLE TO SEE WHO SALUTES IT,** this is a proposal put forward to generate discussion and, you hope, produce a better proposal. It's deliberately imperfect and – as the name suggests – easy to dispose of. The term originated not in anything to do with Guy Fawkes or other combustible figures, but in the development of the computer language Ada in the 1970s: the early 'strawman' draft was followed, as ideas became better thought-out and less liable to change, by woodenman, ironman, tinman and others. In the broader context, a straw man proposal is also known as an Aunt Sally, after the fairground game in which you throw missiles at a target with a view to knocking it over as many times as you like.

Technology migration

The point about a migration, as opposed to a mere upgrade, is that old stuff to which you don't need to refer regularly is stashed away somewhere, so that you can access current material more quickly. One IT website tells us that 'every technology migration project has a starting point in an existing system, and an end game in a new system, and the project is defined by the road that must be travelled to get from the existing system to the new one'. In other words, it is somebody's job to know in advance (but presumably grossly underestimate) the amount of disruption the project will cause.

User-friendly

A self-explanatory – or indeed user-friendly – expression, this means easy to use, designed so that you don't have to be an expert to work out what to do. From its first appearance in the 1970s it took less than a decade to spread beyond the computing world. You can now find 'user-friendly' being applied to anything from life-insurance quotes (= written in plain English) to recipes (= using just a few ingredients and not expecting you to make a chocolate ganache before you start).

Viral marketing

An odd term: you'd think viral marketing would be a bad thing, but no. It can generate massive sales. Since the arrival of social networks, you can tweet information about your product to all your friends, who pass it on to all their friends, who ... Thus, in the twinkling of an eye, everyone knows about it and (in an ideal world) everyone is buying it. It has 'gone viral'. A **SPIN-OFF** of this is that, now that viruses have been rehabilitated, we'll have to come up with a new word for the nasty things that cause swine flu and rabies, but that's a small price to pay for this sort of success.

Following on from this, if any noun can be verbed (see **ACTION**), so apparently can any adjective be nouned. A viral – though not a virus – is now a recognized term for a sales promotion carried out through viral marketing.

Wiki

... is a Hawaiian word meaning 'quick'. Hawaiian is one of those languages where you repeat a word for emphasis, so the name of the original wiki software, WikiWikiWeb, developed by Ward Cunningham of Oregon in the mid-1990s, meant that it was super quick. A wiki – of which the most famous is Wikipedia – is defined (by whom else but Wikipedia itself?) as 'a website that allows the creation and editing of any number of interlinked web pages via a web browser using a simplified markup language or a WYSIWYG text editor'. Ward never patented his idea: he is quoted as saying that he contemplated it but then thought, 'If I got a patent I'd have to go out and sell people on the idea that anyone could edit. That just sounded like something that no one would want to pay money for.' How wrong can you be?

9

Customer value orientation

MARKETING SPEAK

And finally ... all this management is all very well, but you still have to sell the stuff. For that, there is another whole range of vocabulary that may leave the uninitiated baffled.

Big-ticket item

It is, of course, not the ticket (what in the UK might be called the price tag) that is big: it is the price written on it. A big-ticket item is by definition an expensive and non-essential purchase, the sort of product that will be bought only at times of CONSUMER CONFIDENCE. In that sense it has been around – originally in the US – since 1945, but from the time of the American Civil War 'a big ticket' had meant an honourable discharge from the US services. For several hundred years on either side of the Atlantic men discharged from the services or released from prison were given a 'ticket' or warrant to show that they had done their time; in US military parlance a 'small ticket' was a sign that a man had been dishonourably discharged. So a big-ticket item may be expensive and non-essential, but at least it is honourable.

In the early days of the metaphorical use a big-ticket item was usually something like a fridge-freezer. Nowadays we also have 'big-ticket lenders' (banks that will lend £20 million or more as a property investment). In the context of the US federal budget, such 'items' as Medicare and social security, potential victims of swingeing cuts, have also been described as 'big-ticket'. How honourable cutting them may be is another matter.

Brand management

Long-standing senses of the word 'brand' are to do with burning: as early as the sixteenth century a brand was a mark made on a farm animal with a burning iron, to indicate whom it belonged to. From this it became an identifying mark on goods being shipped or marketed, from casks of brandy to consignments of timber. Thence, by the mid-nineteenth century, it became a particular sort of goods, so that you could have a superior brand of anything from ale to candle wax. And so, in the twentieth century, there evolved the concept of the 'brand name' (Cadbury as opposed to Nestlé), the 'brand image' that made the customer think one brand was superior to another and the 'brand manager' whose job it was to promote one particular brand – of chocolate, soap powder, car or whatever – and make sure that the public was aware of it and its individual qualities.

So far, so familiar. The change that has come about in recent years has enabled a person to be a 'brand': Lady Gaga, Jamie Oliver, anyone else of whom the public has a clear image

and who is expected to **DELIVER** at a certain level. Whether the delivery is of outlandish clothes and less outlandish songs or of cheerful recipes for entertaining friends, the public knows what to expect and expects what it knows.

As any brand manager will tell you, however, brands do occasionally need to be 'refreshed', 'repositioned' or 'rebranded'. But you need to get it right. Just as launching a new version of a soft drink when the public liked the old one can be an expensive disaster, so the career of a human 'brand' can crash after, say, an ill-judged appearance on a reality TV show.

Bundling

A bundle, of course, is a number of things loosely wrapped together, like the belongings of a pantomime character carried wrapped in a handkerchief on a pole over the shoulder. But bundling was borrowed into computing to mean selling hardware and software together in the same **PACKAGE** (not, by this time, necessarily a handkerchief), and from there its use extended into other areas of sales and marketing where more than one product or service were supplied together. So a garage selling cars could also provide a 'bundle' that included insurance and a 'free' 10,000km service, while a painter and decorator's 'bundle' could include the provision of carpets and curtains. According to the advocates of bundling, the practice benefits all concerned: the customer has the convenience of 'one-stop shopping' and only one person to complain to if things go wrong, while the seller has the satisfaction of knowing that he has increased his **CUSTOMER VALUE ORIENTATION**.

Commoditization

According to one marketing expert, 'An unrelenting change in technology, in addition to well-informed customers and fast-moving competition, has made sure that many once unique products or services have rapidly lost their intrinsic differentiation value and become "commoditized".' Companies that once enjoyed strong **BRANDING** now find their competitors producing similar or better offerings and suffer from 'the resulting pressure on prices and margins'.

In other words, too many people are making the same sort of stuff, so unless you get your marketing right you are unlikely to make money. The trick is to pursue value-added strategies (see **VAR**), stretch beyond core products and offer customers compellingly differentiated values. But of course you knew that.

Consumer backlash

… means the public taking a dislike to a product, perhaps because it is perceived to be 'too popular'. Heavily oaked Australian chardonnay, for example – *the* thing to drink in the 1980s – fell from favour in the 1990s, probably for no better reason than that it was 'very '80s'. Alternatively, consumers may take against a form of marketing. Being bombarded with random advertisements every time you log on to your email may be so annoying that it turns you against the product being advertised – as a matter of principle, rather than because you have any views on the product itself.

A backlash was originally a jarring movement caused by ill-fitting parts of machinery; by the early twentieth century it had attained its current, figurative meaning of a violent reaction against – well, anything, really, from a political movement to a make of wine.

Consumer confidence

… has been around in the marketing world since the early twentieth century. It is applied either to a specific product that customers will buy because they 'trust' it or to the more general condition of people being prepared to go out and spend money on non-essential, **BIG-TICKET** items – the 'boom' element of a 'boom or bust' economy.

Consumer durable

See **FMCG**.

Consumer headwind

The entertainment group HMV issued a gloomy interim financial statement early in 2011, citing the bad weather before Christmas and the disappointing state of its particular market as reasons for poor sales. It also acknowledged that it was likely to have a difficult few months because of 'well-reported consumer headwinds as we enter 2011'.

This metaphorical meaning hasn't made it into any of my dictionaries – perhaps the HMV spokesperson made it up – but it is easy to see what it means. The poor customer is bravely battling against such difficulties as the credit crunch, increased VAT and the temptation to stay home and shop online (see **FOOTFALL**), just as a cyclist struggles against a strong wind or a football team finds the forces of nature are against it after changing ends at half-time.

Courtesy call

Invariably preceded by the words, 'It's just a …', this ranks high on any list of 'things I don't want to hear' in the modern world. It means that you already subscribe to a service or own a product produced by the caller's company and they want you to buy another, more expensive one (they may call it 'upgrading', but don't be fooled). It's the telephonic equivalent of going into the post office to buy a stamp and being offered home contents insurance and a new credit card at the same time. Grrr.

Critical mass

This is a term from nuclear physics and means 'the minimum mass of fissile material that can sustain a nuclear chain reaction'. It's used in business – mainly by people who wouldn't recognize fissile material if it was handed to them on a large hadron collider – to mean what is needed (in terms of sales or market share) to achieve profitability. Critical mass may also appear in a variety of other contexts: the critical mass of public opinion, for example, might bring about a rethink of government policy; in sociology it means the point at which a change has sufficient momentum to become unstoppable. In physics the expression dates from the 1940s; its wider use is much more recent.

Critical Mass is also the name of several bands, several albums, a couple of video games and a worldwide bicycling event, none of which is relevant here.

Crowdsourcing

An article by Jeff Howe in a 2006 issue of *Wired* magazine described 'the new pool of cheap labor' as 'everyday people using their spare cycles to create content, solve problems, even do corporate R & D'. It went on to say that 'technological advances in everything from product design software to digital video cameras are breaking down the cost barriers that once separated amateurs from professionals ... smart companies in industries as disparate as pharmaceuticals and television [are discovering] ways to tap the latent talent of the crowd.'

This phenomenon is called crowdsourcing (almost invariably without the hyphen that it cries out for) and has rapidly expanded from practical work to various forms of decision-making: the British public was, in 2008, invited to suggest a new flavour for a popular brand of potato crisps. Far from muttering into their cheese and onion that this was what R & D departments were paid for, a million people realized that they had nothing better to do with their time than send bright ideas to the crisp manufacturer. It is as frightening a sign of the times as any expression in this book.

As a matter of interest, I draw your attention to the expression 'spare cycles' at the start of this entry. This has been defined as 'the untapped human potential that explains why Wikipedia has over three and a half million entries in English': blogging and loading the story of their life on to Facebook and YouTube have given many people a creative outlet they have never had before. And why 'cycles'? Well, it's a term from computing and refers to the bits of the computer that can be used to perform function B if it is not working to capacity performing function A. Untapped potential, in other words, which is where we came in.

Customer value orientation

Marketing speak for 'doing what the customer wants'. How well does your organization respond to customer needs? How long does the customer have to wait before receiving the goods or services you provide? Are they generally happy with those goods and services once they receive them? Basically, how good are you at keeping the customer satisfied? Pretty obvious stuff with a fancy name. Notice the absence of a hyphen, which makes the literal meaning harder to analyse: is it 'orientation to give the customer more value' or 'orientation of value specifically for the customer'? Come to think of it, neither of those makes much sense, so perhaps it is better without the hyphen after all.

If, by the way, you work on the basis that the customer is always right, you may not go far wrong but you will be guilty of misquotation. What César Ritz, founder of the Ritz hotels, actually said was, 'The customer is never wrong.' (Well, yes, OK, what he *really* actually said was, '*Le client n'a jamais tort*', but that is nit-picking.) It's a petty distinction, perhaps, but it forms part of a list of 'famous things that were never said', along with 'Play it again, Sam' and 'Come up and see me sometime'.

What Monsieur Ritz thought about *l'orientation du valeur livrée au client* is not recorded. My guess, though, is that he would have thought it was as meaningless in French as it is in English.

Downstream

See **UPSTREAM**.

Elevator pitch

Imagine yourself arriving at work one morning, brimful of a bright new idea. You reach the elevator at just the same moment as the head of department who would have to **BUY INTO** this idea if it were ever to be taken seriously. You almost never have the chance to speak to this person directly – there are several tiers of management between you. Going through

the usual formalities would take months and you would miss the all-important Christmas market. His office is on the twelfth floor. That gives you precisely eighteen seconds to grab his attention and put your idea across.

If you now find yourself goggling at his receding back, you didn't have an elevator pitch.

The word 'pitch' in the sense of 'spiel, sales talk' dates back to 1876 and probably originates in the fairground where the showman's patter was designed to make you part with your nickels and dimes in order to see the bearded lady. The more structured package of proposals that, say, an advertising agency uses in the hopes of winning a contract emerged in the 1960s, and honing your pitch to 'elevator ride' length was popularized in the 1980s. The elevator pitch is now regarded as such a key feature of business and of personal presentation that you can learn it through the Harvard Business School and other distinguished institutions.

It is probably just as well that the concept originated in the US: a 'lift pitch' doesn't have the same ring to it.

End user

When marketing speak created the SUPPLY CHAIN, it also created several tiers of customers. The company that produces components sells them to the company that produces the finished goods (and there may be more than one link in this part of the chain); the manufacturer then sells to a wholesaler who sells to a retailer. All these people are customers of the individual sellers. So when the retailer finally sells to *his* customer – the person who will take the dishwasher home and put dirty dishes in it – that person is distinguished by the title of 'end user', an expression that has been around since the 1960s. If the end user eats or otherwise consumes the product (in which case it is unlikely to be a dishwasher), he may also be a consumer and as such capable of generating CONSUMER BACKLASH or CONSUMER CONFIDENCE.

Focus group

Widely used in all areas of market research, a focus group is a select group of people brought together to *focus* on a given subject or product. The group may be asked what they think of an existing product or, at an earlier stage of development, what they would like the product to **DELIVER**. Unfortunately, focus groups resemble **STAKEHOLDERS** in that their interests are not necessarily aligned: the wishes and opinions of the marketing department, say, may seem completely pie in the sky to the production department whose job it is to deliver the goods.

The idea evolved from the work of American sociologist Robert K Merton (1910–2003) at Columbia University's Bureau of Applied Social Research. According to the *New York Times* obituary:

> His adoption of the focused interview to elicit the responses of groups to texts, radio programs and films led to the 'focus groups' that politicians, their handlers, marketers and hucksters now find indispensable. Long after he had helped devise the **METHODOLOGY**, Mr Merton deplored its abuse and misuse but added, 'I wish I'd get a royalty on it.'

Professor Merton obviously had an eye for a catchy phrase: he is also credited with the invention of the role model and the self-fulfilling prophecy.

Footfall

'People going into shops'. As in 'retailers suffered a dramatic drop in footfall because of the bad weather before Christmas'. In this sense footfall is a coinage from the late 1990s or early 2000s. As far as 'the high street' is concerned it is made particularly relevant not only by people failing to go out in the snow but more permanently by the rise in online shopping. In July 2010 UK shoppers spent £5 billion online, the highest monthly total to date and a year-on-year increase of 18 per cent; experts predict that 2011's total online spending will reach £50 billion. That's a lot of feet that aren't falling anywhere near a shopping mall.

High-end

This is recorded in the US as meaning 'sophisticated, likely to appeal to the wealthy or more discerning buyer' as early as the 1970s. Its opposite is 'low end': 'bottom end' is the same as 'big end', the larger end of a connecting rod in an engine, and need not concern us here. The British equivalents of these terms, 'upmarket' and 'downmarket', were coined at about the same period and for a long time held the Americanisms at bay. Not any more: I recently saw 'high-end' applied to that most British of commodities, marmalade.

(Out of) left field

Baseball again: imagine that you are the batter, standing at the plate and facing the pitcher – the outfielder to your left (about NNW from you) is left field. Because he is in the outfield, he does not play a pivotal role in every phase of the game and may even occasionally **(TAKE HIS) EYE OFF THE BALL**.

The concept of a person being figuratively 'left field' and therefore disconnected with reality dates back to the middle of the twentieth century. From this developed 'a left-field suggestion', meaning a bizarre one; and nowadays a suggestion may also 'come out of left field', meaning that it appears out of nowhere and isn't a logical development of anything that has gone before.

But why should left field be more off the wall, as it were, than right field? Right-handed batters hitting the ball cleanly are likely to send it into left or centre field, so you might think that the right outfielder would be the one who was most adrift from reality. Wikipedia's 'Glossary of English language idioms derived from baseball' (yes, really, there is such a thing) offers several possible explanations, including a complicated one about the legendary Babe Ruth being left-handed and fans buying tickets for the wrong side of the stadium, but frankly they aren't very satisfactory. Perhaps the expression just latches on to the deeply ingrained view that left (= sinister = gauche) is by definition weirder than right.

Managing expectations

All surprises should be good surprises, they say in the PR world, and the best way to achieve this is to under-promise and over-deliver. In other words, work out what you are absolutely confident of being able to achieve, promise a bit less and then do better. Your customers will be thrilled, because you have managed their expectations. But of course they don't know that.

The prime example of managing expectations – attributed to the powers that be at Disneyland – is to put a sign saying, 'Waiting time from here 45 minutes' at the point from which the waiting time is 30 minutes. Customers reach the front of the queue much sooner than they expected, they are delighted, lavish tips proliferate, God's in his heaven and all's right with the world.

Mass sampling

If you've ever bought a magazine with a tiny sachet of moisturizer attached to it, or had a bottle of an unfamiliar brand of mineral water thrust at you at a railway station, you know what mass sampling is, even if you didn't know it had a name. It means handing out samples to the masses, or possibly handing out masses of samples, or both. It's a comparatively recent marketing ploy, common in the FMCG world, to encourage potential customers to try a commodity and, in an ideal world, fall in love with it and buy it avidly for ever more.

Missionary selling

Sounds vaguely risqué, doesn't it? Or might it be something done on a wing and a prayer? In fact, this is a marketing term that has been recognized for twenty years or more, defined as 'selling in which the salesperson's role is to build up goodwill rather than to make a direct sale'. The concept is often applied to a product the customer has never tried before – life insurance, perhaps, or a pension scheme – and is about creating confidence, although obviously with the ultimate end of increasing sales. Why missionary? Well, it's because a missionary seller is going out into uncharted territory, market-wise, with a view to making the heathen masses (= potential new customers) have faith in a new concept. And hoping not to end up in the cooking pot.

Narrowcasting

First there was broadcasting, coined in the 1920s when radio was in its infancy, to mean scattering your message widely to reach the maximum possible audience. Then, shortly afterwards, along came narrowcasting, a system whereby radio signals were not sent out around the full 360 degrees, but restricted to a narrower angle so that programmes were not transmitted to sparsely populated areas. It seems odd in these high-tech days, but presumably it saved money. In this sense the word has more or less died out, only to be revived in the days of cable TV to mean targeting your audience – selling shopping channels to people who are interested in shopping, say, or, as the jargonistas put it, 'niche marketing rather than mass marketing'.

Offer

In the sense of 'an act of offering, something on offer', this goes back five centuries before Mario Puzo's 'offer he can't refuse'. In Newspeak, however, it has become an abbreviation for 'things offered for sale', particularly in the sense of a range of goods that defines a company's image or ethos (see **CORPORATE DNA**). In bookselling terms, for example, a supermarket's 'offer' is very different from that of a specialist bookshop, while a French-style patisserie's 'offer' differentiates it from a café specializing in bacon sandwiches and mugs of tea. This modern sense is so new that is does not appear in the 2008 edition of *Chambers Dictionary* – or perhaps they are merely exercising quality control, not feeling that such a piece of jargon should be part of their own offer.

If you are buying property or contemplating marriage, the word has its own particular – and potentially binding – implications, so be careful how you use it.

Penetration

Whatever other implications this word may have, in marketing speak it is entirely desirable but completely unconnected with sex (see **MISSIONARY SELLING** for another example of an expression that isn't smutty after all). It has been used since the 1960s to describe the extent to which a product or innovation has been sold into a particular market. Susan Wojcicki of Google, talking about new marketing opportunities for her organization, was quoted in 2010 as saying, 'These smartphones have not been around for that long … Penetration is still growing.' Meaning, presumably, that not everyone has bought one yet, but they soon will have.

Prosumer

Prosumers – an amalgam of producers and consumers – were coined by 'futurist' Alvin Toffler in his 1980 book *The Third Wave*. By 'third wave' he meant the post-industrial society that was in its infancy at the time, following the first and second waves of agricultural and industrial society. In an agricultural society, Toffler maintained, everyone was a prosumer – they

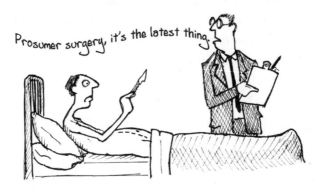

grew their own food, built their own home, etc. Once they began to produce a surplus (the beginnings of industrialization), more and more people became consumers, buying things that other people had produced. The development of the marketplace produced a very different society in which everyone was dependent on everyone else: 'The failure of a major steel mill or glass factory to deliver needed supplies to an auto plant could, under certain circumstances, send repercussions throughout a whole industry or regional economy.'

Are you with me so far? OK, now we hit the decline of industrialization and the birth of the technological age. And all sorts of interesting things happen. People have more leisure, so they take up DIY. Putting together a flatpack from IKEA – doing part of the job for the producer – is a form of prosumerism. Technology advances. Toffler cites the home pregnancy test as an early example of people taking some of their health care into their own hands: previously such a test had had to be done by a doctor or lab technician. Self-help groups grow up. People wanting to give up smoking, or worried about their bad eating habits, or finding being the parents of twins exhausting, go not to the doctor or a paid therapist, but to a support group organized by fellow 'sufferers'. They are going back to a form of self-sufficiency, shifting from being 'passive consumer to active prosumer'.

Toffler predicted many of the changes that have taken place over the last thirty years, but he didn't quite envisage the phenomenon of **WIKI**, which takes prosumerism a stage further. As executive coach James Caplin puts it in his book *I Hate Presentations* (2008), 'We used to have encyclopedias. They, the knowledgeable, shared their wisdom with us, the ignorant. It was an adult-to-child interaction. We now have Wikipedias. We, the knowledgeable ones, share our information with each other.' In the twenty-first century we are back where our ancestors were over a thousand years ago: we are not only productive but **PROACTIVE** consumers.

Pull marketing

The old-fashioned approach was sometimes called 'push marketing' – you got out there into the marketplace, told people how wonderful your stuff was and they bought it. Pull marketing is more subtle than that. It lures the customer in with 'buy me now' offers that sound like a bargain ('two for the price of one') but also give a sense of urgency ('while stocks last', 'must end Friday'). This idea has really come into its own since the invention of online networking: potential clients can visit your website, read your blog, take note of your special offers and decide that yours is the sort of company they want to do business with. Won't you come into my parlour, as the spider said to the fly.

Real time

In the early days of computing, doing something 'in real time' meant there and then, giving results more or less instantly rather than analysing or processing them later. Latterly the term has been adopted by the marketing world, so that 'real-time marketing' means 'responding very quickly to the needs of the marketplace or customer'. The blurb for David Meerman Scott's book *Real-time Marketing and PR: How to Instantly Engage Your Market, Connect with Customers, and Create Products That Grow Your Business Now* (2010) explains it with remarkably little claptrap and a commendable absence of exclamation marks: 'Gone are the days when you could plan out your marketing and public relations programs well in advance and release them on your timetable. It's a real-time world now, and if you're not engaged, then you're on your way to marketplace irrelevance. "Real time" means news breaks over minutes, not days. It means ideas percolate, then suddenly and unpredictably go VIRAL to a global audience ... it's when businesses see an opportunity and are the first to act on it.'

So what are you sitting here for? Get out there.

Running it up the flagpole

In the film *Twelve Angry Men*, set in a jury room, one of the jurors is a brash young advertising man who tells a story about **BRAINSTORMING** sessions at his agency. When a deadlock arises, one of his colleagues will always say, 'Here's an idea. Let's run it up the flagpole and see if anyone salutes it.' The character relating this thinks it is a marvellous example of **THINKING OUTSIDE THE BOX**: 'I mean, it's idiotic,' he says admiringly, 'but it's funny, huh?'

That was in 1957 and clearly the image – meaning to float an idea, to see if anyone thinks it is any good – was new to the other jurors he was talking to. Nowadays you don't have to use the full expression for people to know what you mean: a sure sign that it has descended into the realms of cliché.

Later in the film, the same indefatigably cheerful character comes up with another idea, which he prefaces with, 'Let's throw it out on the stoop and see if the cat licks it up', an expression which seems, mercifully, not to have caught on. And, maybe it was just Hollywood, maybe it was that line of work that required lots of variations on the same theme, but in the 1962 film *Days of Wine and Roses* a PR executive suggests that he 'pull something out of the hat and see if it hops for us'. Was it the innate hint of patriotism that made 'run it up the flagpole' win out against this strong competition?

Spin

Baseball pitchers put a spin on the ball to control its direction and make it more difficult for the batter to 'read'. This may be where the modern sense – of putting a particular slant on a piece of news or government policy – originated: the person doing the spinning controls where the information goes and how it is interpreted. The expression emerged in American politics in the late 1970s, but was soon adopted by the British. Political public relations officers were rebranded as 'spin doctors' shortly afterwards. Why 'doctor' (as opposed to, say, 'artist', by analogy with 'con artist'), it is difficult to say, but it is worth noting that 'to doctor' in the sense of 'to alter the appearance of, to tamper with or "cook"' has been in use since the eighteenth century and shows no signs of going away.

Supply chain

The supply chain originated in military parlance: it was the route by which an army received its supplies. In that sense it is over a hundred years old. Its use in the business context dates back to the 1950s: ever since then it has meant the chain of processes involved in the production of a commodity and its journey towards its **END USER**. See also **DELIVERY** and **UPSTREAM/ DOWNSTREAM**.

Upstream/downstream

By the 1970s these words were no longer confined to rivers; they had spread out into the oil industry to describe the 'flow' of the various stages of the process. The upstream elements are exploration and research and the downstream ones refining, distribution and marketing. Nowadays, upstream or downstream activities can take place in any business, either within a corporation or between a number of companies which form part of the same SUPPLY CHAIN. Within a corporation, an upstream loan, for example, is a loan from a subsidiary company to its holding company, given because the latter doesn't have a good enough credit rating to borrow money elsewhere. In the supply-chain context, upstream refers to the manufacturers of components and suppliers of materials; downstream from them are those who put the components together and then the various levels of customers under finally, most downstream of all, is the END USER.

Acknowledgements

When I started talking about writing this book, a number of friends said, 'Oh, you must include ...', normally followed by 'That really annoys me.' So building up a contents list was, as it has been before, a communal effort. Particular thanks are due this time to Alex, Carol and Lorraine for working in the sort of jobs where this vocabulary is rampant. Thanks also to Louise, Ana and everyone else at Michael O'Mara for continuing to fire on all cylinders.

Bibliography

This book couldn't have been written without the brilliant people who compile the *Oxford English Dictionary* and the kind ones at Westminster Libraries who allow me to view it online. Many of the definitions are based on my beloved *Chambers Dictionary* 2008, the *Collins English Dictionary* and the online *Merriam-Webster Dictionary* (www.merriam-webster.com).

I have also drawn inspiration and information from the following books and sites.

James Caplin, *I Hate Presentations* (Capstone, 2008)

Julia Cresswell, *The Cat's Pyjamas: the Penguin Book of Clichés* (Penguin, 2007)

Simon Ellis & Janet Tod, *Behaviour for Learning* (Routledge, 2009)

Brian Fugere, Chelsea Hardaway & Jon Warshawsky, *Why Business People Speak Like Idiots: a bullfighter's guide* (Free Press, 2005)

Jonathon Green, *Dictionary of Jargon* (Routledge & Kegan Paul 1987)

Kamran Kashani (ed.), *Beyond Traditional Marketing* (Wiley, 2005)

David Meerman Scott, *Real-time Marketing and PR* (Wiley, 2010)

Ron Sturgeon, *Green Weenies and Due Diligence* (Mike French Publishing, 2005)

Alvin Toffler, *The Third Wave* (Collins, 1980)

Tony Thorne, *Shoot the Puppy* (Penguin Reference, 2006)

Clive Whichelow & Hugh Murray, *It's Not Rocket Science and Other Irritating Modern Clichés* (Portrait, 2007)

www.jrank.org/business

www.phrases.org.uk/meanings

http://searchenterprisewan.techtarget.com

Index

A
action 89
agile development 143
American football terminology 60
animal metaphors
    cash cows 20, 132
    cubicle monkeys 12–13, 84
    dead cat bounce 135
    ducks in a row 13
    elephant in the room 13–14
    nibbled to death by ducks 80
    one-trick pony 82
    shooting the puppy 31–2
anti-trust 128
art, state of the 48–9
asset-purchasing 142
asset-stripping 129, 142

B
B2B (business to business)
    113–14
ballpark 129–30
bandwagon effect 75–6
bar, raising the 29
base, touching 25, 33
baseball terminology 33, 38–9,
    62–3, 129–30, 172–3
bases, covering all 38–9
batting on a sticky wicket 15
BCP (business continuity plan)
    115
bed with, get into 90
being on the same page 47–8
benchmark 53–4
big end 171
big picture 53, 54, 55, 78

big-ticket item 158–9, 163
biting the bullet 32
black-box accounting 130–31
Black Friday 131–2
blamestorming 77
bleeding edge 39
blue-sky thinking 36–7
BOGOF (buy one, get one free)
    114
bottom end 171
bottom line 132
bottom-up 109
bowling terminology 13
box, thinking outside the 36, 38,
    49, 180
boxing terminology 46
BPCP (business process
    contingency plan) 115
brain dump 9–10
brainstorming 37–8, 76, 180
brand management 96, 159–60,
    161
broad brush 55
broke, if it ain't 23, 36, 78–9
broker 90–91
brownie points 10–11, 58
bullet, biting the 32
bundling 27, 161
buttons, pushing someone's 28
buying into 91, 167

C
caffeine-fuelled 38
car terminology see vehicle
    terminology
cash cows 20, 133

CBD (central business district) 115
click of a mouse, at the 144
close of play 11
closure 145
cloud-based 146–7
coming from, I know/ see where you are 55, 77
commoditization 161–2
computer terminology 143–57
  black-box 130–31
  DRP 115–16
  hands-on 61–2
  real time 179
  user-friendly 14
  WYSIWYG 127
considering your position 11
consumer backlash 162–3, 169
consumer confidence 158, 163, 169
consumer durable 117
consumer headwind 163–4
core competencies 92
corporate DNA 56
cost driver 134
counted, stand up and be 72
courtesy call 164
covering all bases 38–9
creative accounting 131, 134–5
cricket terminology 11, 15, 29–30
critical mass 164–5
crowdsourcing 165–6
cubicle monkeys 12–13, 84
curve, learning 43–4, 110
customer value orientation 161, 166 7
cutting edge 39
cyberspace 147
cycles, spare 166
cylinders, firing on all 30, 41

D
dashboards 56–7
dead cat bounce 135

deal, done 135
delayering 92
delivery 93, 96, 160, 170
diligence, due 136–7
direct reports 54, 77, 93–4
discrimination 17, 18–19
DNA, corporate 56
done deal 135
don't fight the tape 136
double-dip 136
downshifting 40
downsizing 11, 16, 24, 32, 57, 92, 100
downstream 182
drawing a line under it 11, 58, 98
DRP (disaster recovery planning) 16, 115–16
ducks in a row 13
ducks, nibbled to death by 80
due diligence 136–7
dynamic 94–5

E
elephant in the room 13–14
elevator pitch 167–9
empowerment 35, 95, 101, 112
end user 93, 169, 181, 182
engagement 96
engineering terminology
  benchmark 53–4
  black-box 130–31
  dynamic 94
  firing on all cylinders 41
  pushing the envelope 46–7
  state of the art 48–9
entry level 14, 15
envelope, pushing the 36, 38, 39, 46–7
ETA 28, 116–17
ethnicity 18–19
executive decisions 58
expectations, managing 173
eye off the ball, taking your 15, 172

F

face time 96–7, 112, 148
facilitator 97
fast-track 15
film industry 54
fire-fighting 16, 115
firing on all cylinders 30, 41
fit for purpose 41–2
flagpole, running it up the 155, 180
FMCG (fast-moving consumer goods) 117–18, 174
focus group 170
footfall 171
forum 147–8
forward, going 98
FPO 119
front line 93
front-line services 59
FUD (fear, uncertainty and doubt) 118–19
functional flexibility 97

G

gagging clause 16–17
game plan 60
game, raising the 29
game theory 51, 66, 73
gardening leave 17–18, 20, 44
gatekeeper 148
get with the programme 32, 44, 45
glass ceiling 17, 18–19
goalposts, moving the 11, 19, 25
going forward 98
golden boy 20
golden handcuffs 20
golden handshakes 19–20, 32
golden hellos 20
golden parachutes 20
graduate calibre 14, 21
grasping the nettle 32
guesstimate 130, 137
guidelines 60, 68

H

hands-on/ hands-off 61–2
hands, safe pair of 15, 29
hard-wired 148
hardball, playing 62–3
heads-up 21–2
hear what you say, I 77, 78
high-end 171
hitting the ground running 14, 22–3, 30, 42
horizontal initiative 98–9
horse racing terminology 15, 32, 63
hymn sheet, singing from the same 47–8

I

I hear what you say 77, 78
I know/ see where you are coming from 55, 77
if it ain't broke, don't fix it 23, 36, 78–9
in real terms 70
in the loop 32, 152
information design 149
information overload 52, 150
input 151
IPO (initial public offering) 119–20

J

joined-up 42–3

K

keeping your options open 63–4, 65
knee-jerk reaction 23
knowledge base 151
KPIs (Key Performance Indicators) 21, 56, 120–21
KSFs (key success factors) 121

L

leading edge 39
learning curve 43–4, 110
left field, out of 172
let go 16, 22, 24, 27, 44, 58
level playing field 25
leverage 137–8
licence to print money 138–9,
    141
lifecycle assessment/costing
    139–40
lipstick index/lipstick indicator
    140
loop, in the 32, 95, 152
lose-lose situation 66
low end 171

M

malware 152
managing expectations 173
marzipan layer 17, 19, 20, 25–6
mass sampling 174
mathematical terminology 68,
    72, 73
MBWA (management by
    wandering around) 121–2
medical origins 23, 37, 45
message, on 32, 44, 48
methodologies 26, 68, 130, 143,
    170
micro-management 30, 54, 55,
    79
migration, technology 155
military terminology
    big-ticket 158–9
    front-line services 59
    heads-up 21
    mission statement 64–5
    parapets (above the/below the)
        39, 69
    supply chain 181
mindset 27
mission statement 64–5
missionary selling 174

money, license to print 138–9,
    141
monitoring the situation 65
monkeys, cubicle 12–13, 84
mouse, click of a 144
movers and shakers 30, 65–6
moving the goalposts 11, 19, 25
mushroom management 13,
    79–80

N

narrowcasting 175
nerve centre 45
nettle, grasping the 32
nibbled to death by ducks 80
no-win situation 66

O

OEM 122–3
offer 48, 175–6
on message 32, 44, 48
one-trick pony 82
open-door management 77,
    99–100
options open, keeping your 63–4,
    65
orphan 15, 152–3
outsourcing 100
overload, information 52
ownership 35, 100–101

P

package 27
page, being on the same 47–8
pan out 67
paradigm shift 67–8, 114
parameters 68
parapets (above the/below the)
    39, 69
paywall 153
penetration 115, 176
performance coaching 101
play, close of 11
playing field, level 25

playing hardball 62–3
political terminology
    executive decision 58
    front-line services 59
    joined-up 42–3
    on message 44
    stand up and be counted 72
    way forward 110–11
Ponzi scheme 141
position, considering your 11
proactive 101–2, 108, 178
procurement 154
programme, get with the 32, 44,
    45
prosumer 176–7
psychology terminology 44, 101
pull marketing 178–9
punching above your weight 46
puppy, shooting the 31–2
purpose, fit for 41–2
pushing someone's buttons 28
pushing the envelope 36, 38, 39,
    46–7

Q
quality-driven 104
quantitative easing 141–2
quantum leap 47

R
raising the bar 29
raising your game 29
rationalizing 103
RBM (results-based management)
    123
real terms, in 70
real time 179
reinventing the wheel 83
reports, direct 54, 77
resource allocation 104
results-driven 104
revenue streams 105, 114
revolving-door policy 83–4
ring-fencing 70–71

running, hitting the ground 14,
    22–3, 30, 42
running it up the flagpole 155,
    180

S
safe pair of hands 15, 29
salami tactics 79, 84
sampling, mass 174
scenario, worst-case 87–8
scientific terminology 47, 48–9
    corporate DNA 56
    critical mass 164–5
    dynamic 94
    paradigm shifts 67–8
    quantum leap 47
    state of the art 48–9
self-starters 30, 101
shoe to drop, waiting for the other
    86
shooting the puppy 31–2
shower, thought 37–8
singing from the same song
    sheet/hymn sheet 47–8
sitting down 71
skill set 105
SMB (small and medium-sized
    business) 123–4
song sheet, singing from the same
    47–8
spare cycles 166
speed, up to 32
spin 27, 44, 118, 181
spin-offs/spin-outs 71, 156
sports terminology
    ballpark 129–30
    batting on a sticky wicket 15
    covering all bases 38–9
    fast-track 15
    game plan 60
    horses for courses 63
    level playing field 25
    moving the goalposts 18, 25
    out of left field 172–3